Pearson's Canal Co...
FOUR COUNTIES
including the whole of the Trent & ... Canal

IBEX
BRITISH WATERWAYS
215

Published by
Central Waterways Supplies
Rugby, Warks CV21 2NP
Tel/fax 01788 546692
email: sales@centralwaterways.co.uk
Eighth edition 2007. ISBN 978 0 9 5491168 3

Tîllerman

How appropriate, how serendipitous, that this eighth edition of *Pearson's Canal Companion to the Four Counties Ring* should burst forth from its cocoon exactly twenty-five years after the prototype first appeared to polite, if muted, applause. The original was as slender as its author: and both have grown in size - and wisdom too; or so I would like to think.

That first Companion broke several moulds and shibboleths in canal guide book design and format: the route it covered was circular and the maps were so arranged that users could progress in a clockwise or anti-clockwise manner throughout their journey without the need to reconfigure at each nodal point; the book was landscape in format with a running commentary on the passing scene aligned - in most cases - above the map, with an accompanying gazetteer of places and facilities below. A sequence of mini-features appeared at intervals to leaven the mood and avoid monotony. Apart from the front cover, the photography was black & white, whilst the maps were printed black and brown on cream paper, giving the book a wistful air which appeared to go down well with its intended audience.

But we are a race of pigeon-holers and in double-quick time the Canal Companions were deemed hire-boater fodder. Of self-appointedly superior caste, private boaters clung to their tedious, inaccurate and out of date Nicholsons like Nonconformists wary of the New Testament. It took a long time to debunk their misconceptions, and we did not really claim our crown until publication of *Pearson's Canal Companion to the Birmingham Canal Navigations* seven years later. That was the first of our sign-written covers and Brian Collings has 'docked' fifty mini-masterpieces since, somehow contriving to come up with fresh colour schemes and liveries, many echoing real life applications from the past on boats, buses and trains.

And you will be wanting to know what I have learned from quarter of a century of canal guide research and production! Well I know that our canals are an increasingly rich and valuable resource in a country where space is at a premium; but that, more tellingly, they are not always recognised as such by the powers that be. Budgetary considerations are apt to outweigh common sense; planning is piecemeal and strategies short-term. I believe that many more miles of towpath are worthy of the Sustrans treatment; I would like to see all towns and cities providing well-lit and welcoming moorings for visiting boaters; I should like to see far more than lip-service paid to our canalside heritage; and I still fervently believe that modern short-haul transport by water has an increasingly important environmental and commercial role to play.

Projections based on past performance are not always reliable, if they were then the Canal Companions of 2032 will consist of 192 pages and cost £35. Whether I will still be compiling them is, of course, a matter for conjecture - though not something I would necessarily advise you to bet against!

Michael Pearson

you are looking for
boating holiday you
eed look no further

Hire direct from the leading narrowboat
operators with all boats inspected and
awarded star ratings by Visit Britain.

leet of over 200 boats for 2 to 12 people
m 11 start bases throughout the UK so
u can be sure of the widest choice.

ginners are welcome.

sit our website or telephone for a free brochure

0845 126 4098

ww.ukboathire.com

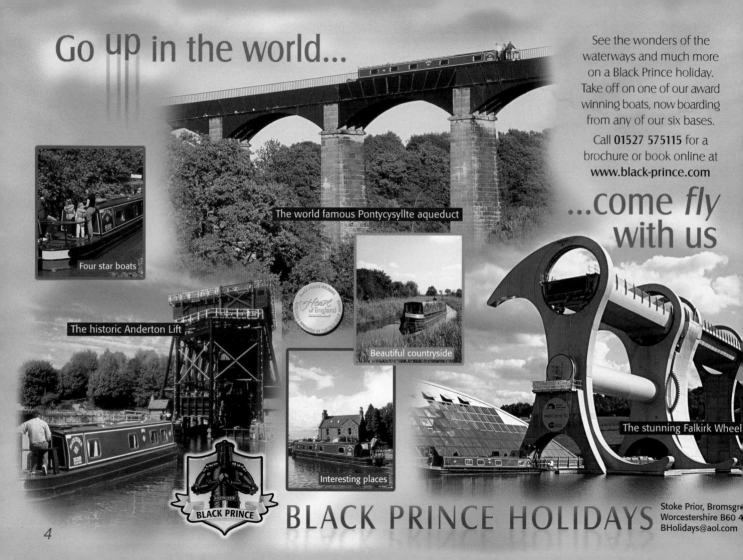

4

The Trent & Mersey Canal

Weston Cliffs

THE junction between the Trent & Mersey and Bridgewater canals lies, somewhat mysteriously, a few yards inside the northern end of Preston Brook Tunnel. Walking the old horse path over the top of the tunnel, you'll come upon milepost 92 in the sequence from Shardlow, the canal's southern terminus. The tunnel isn't wide enough for narrow boats to pass inside, and access is controlled by a timetable - southbound boats may enter for ten minutes on the half hour; northbound similarly on the hour. Neither is it exactly straight - being one of the earliest canal tunnels it seems that Brindley had yet to perfect the art of digging in a direct line.

At the southern end of the tunnel the Trent & Mersey Company built a stop lock to protect their water supply from being drawn into the Bridgewater Canal. Nearby stands a drydock covered by a valanced canopy which has a distinct railway character. No surprise, for the dock was built by the North Staffordshire Railway - one time owners of the canal - for the maintenance of steam tugs introduced in 1865 to haul boats through the tunnel in the absence of a towpath.

Between Dutton Lock and Bartington Wharf the canal hugs the shoulders of the Weaver Valley, making its way awkwardly across the armpits of a sequence of wooded ravines which must have challenged the canal builder's patience. From time to time these (bluebell-filled in Spring) woods recede, and there are glimpses to be had of the neighbouring Weaver Navigation, sadly now bereft of commercial shipping, but until relatively recently a busy outlet for the products of mid-Cheshire's salt and chemical industries. On the skyline beyond Dutton Locks looms an imposing railway viaduct - it carries the West Coast Main Line over the valley. Sixty feet high and totalling twenty arches, it dates from 1837 and is the work of Joseph Locke.

Bridgewater Canal from Manchester

Willow Green 207

Holly Bush

pipe

A49

forge
Bartington Wharf

208

209

210 mp

70'

Black Prince

Acton Bridge

70'

211

mp

212

213

Dutton Locks

The towpath is mostly wide and flat, though sometimes grassy along this length. Comfortable for walkers, not always so for cyclists!

Weaver Navigation to Weston Point

Dutton
Stop
Lock

drydock

70'

70'

mp

Claymoore Navigation Midland Chandlers

former flour warehouse

55'

mp

Dutton
Tunnel Top

Preston Brook Tunnel *1239 yrds*

industrial estate

Spar

Preston Brook

A56 to Chester   A533 to Runcorn

Summary of Facilities
There is a Spar convenience store within easy reach of the canal at Preston Brook whilst a pub called the TUNNEL TOP (Tel: 01928 718181) stands above Preston Brook Tunnel.

Three pubs lie close to Bridge 209: THE HORNS (Tel: 01606 852192), the LEIGH ARMS (Tel: 01606 853327) and the HOLLY BUSH (Tel: 01606 853196). Would-be patrons should exercise extreme care, however, as the A49's traffic is fast, furious and unforgiving.

THE Trent & Mersey revels in its remarkably lovely journey through a rural landscape of rolling farmland interspersed with belts of deciduous woodland, eventually becoming engulfed in the dusky portals of Saltersford and Barnton tunnels. In common with Preston Brook they are just not wide enough to enable narrow boats to pass inside, but on this occasion they are short enough to be negotiated without delay to oncoming traffic. A broad leafy pool, much favoured by fishermen, separates the two tunnels and the old horse-paths continue to provide walkers with a bosky connecting link across the tops.

Of all the so-called "Seven Wonders of the Waterways", ANDERTON LIFT is arguably the most ingenious. It performs its role of raising or lowering craft through the fifty feet disparity in level between the Trent & Mersey Canal and Weaver Navigation. The Lift dates from 1875 and was designed by Edwin Clark. Its imposing framework contains two water-filled caissons, each capable of holding a pair of narrowboats. Corrosion of the metalwork brought about its closure in 1983, and it remained embarrassingly out of use for the best part of twenty years. With £7 million of Heritage Lottery funding it re-opened in 2002, a star visitor attraction in its own right, never mind its strategic importance in linking the canal with the Weaver.

continued on page 8

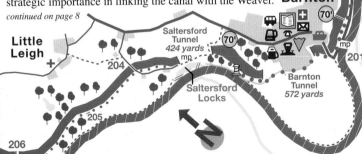

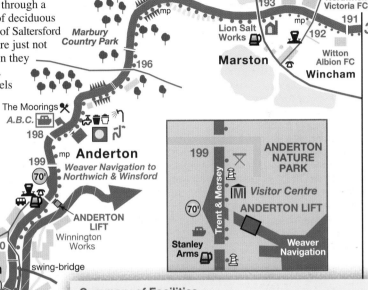

Summary of Facilities

Barnton (best approached from the north portal of Barnton Tunnel) is well served with shops including general stores, a butcher, post office, two chemists and a Chinese takeaway. There is also a useful post office store at Anderton.

There are several pubs along this length, most obviously the STANLEY ARMS (Tel: 01606 75059) opposite Anderton Lift and the SALT BARGE (Tel: 01606 43064) across the road from Lion Salt Works at Bridge 193. THE MOORINGS (Tel: 01606 79789) is located at Anderton Marina and offers lunch and dinner.

Frequent buses run from both Barnton and Anderton to and from Northwich town centre. Tel: 01244 602666.

continued from page 7

East of Anderton the Trent & Mersey winds past Marbury Country Park largely untouched by the outskirts of Northwich, though there are occasional glimpses of the town and its chemical industry nestling down in the valley of the Weaver. Centuries of salt production has destabilised the landscape. In 1958 a new length of canal had to be dug at Marston to by-pass a section troubled by subsidence. Eastwards, the horizon is dominated by the substantial parish church at Great Budworth.

Lion Salt Works was the last in Britain still producing salt by the process of evaporation in open brine pans. By the mid Eighties it was struggling to compete with more up to date mass production techniques before it finally went out of business. In the years since then a number of

Boat dock near Preston Brook

One of the Trent & Mersey's famous 'flashes' near Higher Shurlach

attempts have been made to have it restored as a working museum. It has even featured in BBC's popular *Restoration* programme, but progress appears decidedly slow. In its heyday the works operated its own small fleet of narrowboats plying between Marston and Anderton where the salt would be transhipped into larger vessels for export through the Mersey ports.

Between bridges 191 and 192 the canal is sandwiched between the stadia of two non-league football teams: Northwich Victoria founded in 1874; and Witton Albion founded in 1887. Two football clubs of considerable tradition, yet with an average combined core spectatorship of less than two thousand, possessed of modern grounds separated solely by a canal - doesn't that illustrate the grandeur and folly of football perfectly!

PREDOMINANTLY rural in character, the Trent & Mersey Canal makes its way through the peaceful valley of the River Dane, only the suburbs of Broken Cross and the ICI works at Lostock contrive to break the bucolic spell. The most curious feature of this section of the canal are the subsidence-induced flashes bordering the main channel to the south of Bridge 181. That nearest the bridge was once filled with the submerged wrecks of abandoned narrowboats, an inland waterway equivalent of Scapa Flow. Many of the boats were brought here and sunk en masse during the Fifties in circumstances almost as controversial in canal terms as the scuttling of the German fleet at Scapa after the First World War. In what was probably a book-keeping exercise, British Waterways rid themselves of surplus narrowboats in a number of watery graves throughout the system. In recent years all the wrecks have been raised and taken off for restoration: one generation's cast-offs become the next's prized possessions. Hereabouts the Dane, nearing journey's end at Northwich where it joins the Weaver, has grown sluggish with age, meandering about its level valley in a succession of broad loops, so that at one moment it is hard by the canal, the next away across the fields of milking herds. The soil here is soft and the river carves deep banks shadowed by alder and willow. By way of piquant contrast, in the environs of Higher Shurlach sweet aromas issue forth from Roberts Bakery.

Keep to Channel !

River Dane

Whatcroft Hall

Orchard Marina

Broken Cross

Higher Shurlach

Wincham Wharf

lagoons

Old Broken Cross

Canal Shop

bakery

chemical works

Rudheath

pipes

Northwich - Sandbach (goods only)

176 177 178 179 181 182 182A 183 184 185 186 189 4

Summary of Facilities

Two attractive pubs punctuate your progress along this length of canal. THE WHARF at Wincham (Tel: 01606 46099) is a warehouse conversion located alongside Bridge 189. In contrast, the OLD BROKEN CROSS (Tel: 01606 40431) by Bridge 184 is a long established, but refurbished, boatman's inn offering a good range of food. Also by Bridge 184 is a canal shop.

There are fish & chip and Chinese takeaways west of Bridge 189. West of Bridge 184, Northwich station lies approximately a mile from the canal. A large Tesco superstore (open 24 hours) stands alongside the station.

MIDDLEWICH is one of those arcane places well-known in canal circles but meaningless to most other people. In the old days it was salt which brought so much traffic to Middlewich's canals; the salt boats and, of course, the coal boats without which industry could not function in that pre-electric age. Now, though, it's with pleasure boating that this small town is predominantly concerned, with two hire fleets and a boatyard adding traffic to the often frenetically busy Trent & Mersey Canal.

Five locks punctuate the canal's progress around the eastern edge of the town. The central three - deep and tediously slow to use - are bordered by compounds of stacked pallets and the baleful architecture of small industrial units; all a far cry from the salty scenes of the past, when Seddons and Cerebos were at their zenith and a forest of flaring chimney stacks appeared to support the Middlewich sky.

North of the town, Croxton Aqueduct carries the canal over the River Dane, not far from its confluence with the Wheelock. Originally the aqueduct was built to broad-beam dimensions. Close inspection of the undergrowth reveals some remnants of the old supporting piers. Now, ironically, it is just about the narrowest place between Preston Brook and Middlewich.

Big Lock lives up to its name, recalling the original concept that the canal be capable of handling widebeam craft inland from the Mersey ports as far as Middlewich: that, at least, was the idea, until someone decided to skimp on the tunnels.

Every time we come here, Town Wharf is still 'To Let'. Strange and sad how some former canal buildings seem so ripe for redevelopment whilst others are stifled and moribund.

Middlewich Narrowboats' hire base and boatyard, with its old canal managers' house and attractive canopy, strikes a welcome element of dignity. Their drydock was once used by Seddons to maintain their fleet of narrowboats.

Bridge 168 spans what is ostensibly the Shropshire Union Canal's Middlewich Branch, though the first hundred yards were actually built by the Trent & Mersey in a ruse to extract increased tolls. Keep an eye on boat movements here for Middlewich can suddenly become Muddlewich when someone comes shooting out of the Shropshire Union without advance warning. More interesting industries line the canal as it escapes, southwards, from the town: a sanitaryware factory, British Salt, and not least the Bisto gravy works!

Map labels:
- chemical works 68
- 67 161
- (70') 162
- 163
- Booth Lane Locks 28ft 9ins
- 69
- 164
- 165
- RHM
- British Salt 70
- sanitaryware works
- Rumps Lock 9ft 2ins
- 166
- Middlewich Locks 32ft 7ins
- Kings Lock 11ft 3ins
- 73
- 72
- 169
- 71
- 172
- 74 mp
- 168
- Wardle Lock 9ft 9ins
- 4.C.R.
- Big Lock 5ft 0ins 75
- River Dane
- 31
- 30
- **Middlewich**
- (70')
- 29
- 28
- mp A530
- 173
- aqueducts
- **Keep to Channel !**
- 175
- A533
- **3**
- Croxton Aqueduct
- River Wheelock
- Stanthorne Lock 11ft 1in
- 27
- 45
- A530 to Nantwich

Inset map (MIDDLEWICH):
- drydock
- chandlery
- Kings Lock
- (70')
- 169
- Andersen Boats
- Middle-168 wich Narrow-boats
- 167
- 31
- **MIDDLEWICH**

*Figures refer to Trent & Mersey

Middlewich *(Map 4)*

A salt making town since Roman days, Middlewich's most interesting building is the parish church of St Michael whose tower is scarred with missiles unleashed during the Civil War - apparently they are still trying to sort out the insurance.

Eating & Drinking

BIG LOCK - canalside Big Lock. Good range of beers, bar meals and a la carte menu. Canalside seating area. Tel: 01606 833489.
KINGS LOCK - canalside Kings Lock. Food and accommodation. Tel: 01606 833537.
KINGS LOCK FISH & CHIPS - canalside Kings Lock. Tel: 01606 832020.
NEWTON BREWERY INN - canalside south of Big Lock. Old fashioned Marston's local. Tel: 01606 833502.
KINDERTONS - hotel/restaurant adjacent Bridge 172. Tel: 01606 834325.
SPICE GARDEN - canalside Rumps Lock. Tel: 01606 841549. Indian restaurant/take-away housed in former canalside pub.

Shopping

Old-fashioned shops make this a pleasant town to restock the galley. There's a Somerfield supermarket, as well as branches of NatWest and Barclays banks. A small market is held each Tuesday, whilst a number of shops close at midday on Wednesdays.

Connections

BUSES - Arriva service 37 links Middlewich with Sandbach and Crewe (for the railway station) Tel: 0870 608 2 608.

Sandbach *(Map 5)*

Chiefly famous for its ancient Saxon crosses, Sandbach lies about a mile east of the canal at Ettily Heath, though there is easy access to the railway station from Bridge 160. In transport circles Sandbach is lauded as the home of lorry making. Fodens had their roots in 19th century agricultural machinery and they were at the forefront of the development of steam lorries. Edwin Richard Foden (ERF) broke away from the family business to concentrate on diesel lorries

Middlewich

and, seeing how successful he became, the family followed suit. You cannot drive very far nowadays without meeting a modern juggernaut built by one or other of these firms. Buses as Middlewich.

Wheelock *(Map 5)*

Although by-passed by the A534, Wheelock still endures more than its fair share of traffic - a culture shock after the peace of the canal. Nevertheless, it's a useful pitstop with a newsagent, convenience store, pet food superstore and post office selling canal souvenirs. Refreshment opportunities are plentiful: try the CHESHIRE CHEESE (Tel: 01270 760319), the CAMRA recommended and wonderfully unspoilt COMMERCIAL HOTEL (Tel: 01270 760122), the canalside OLD MILL RESTAURANT (Tel: 01270 762030), or LIZ'S PLAICE fish & chip shop (Tel: 01270 768114). Buses as Middlewich.

Hassall Green *(Map 5)*

Isolated community somewhat impinged upon by the M6. But there are still pleasant walks to be had along country lanes. Downhill, past the mission church painted shocking pink, the old North Staffordshire Railway has been converted into the "Salt Line" bridleway. There's a pottery adjacent to Bridge 146. Refreshments are available at the LOCK 57 CAFE/BRASSERIE (Tel: 01270 762266) or at the ROMPING DONKEY (Tel: 01270 765202), a country pub only a few hundred yards north of Bridge 147. The canalside post office stores stocks a moderate selection of groceries plus a good range of canal souvenirs, books, maps etc. Various boating facilities - diesel, Calor Gas, logs and coal - are also available here.

LOCKS proliferate, and are potentially habit-forming, as the Trent & Mersey ascends from (or descends to) the Cheshire Plain. There are twenty-six chambers to negotiate in only seven miles between Wheelock and Hardings Wood, and "Heartbreak Hill" - as this section has been known to generations of boaters - seems an all too appropriate nickname by the time you have reached the top or bottom; 250 feet up or down.

With the exception of the PIERPOINT pair, all the locks were 'duplicated' in the 1830s, paddles between adjoining chambers enabling one lock to act as a mini-reservoir to its neighbour. These side paddles were taken out of use when commercial traffic ceased towards the end of the 1960s, but the duplicated locks still ease delays today, though on our most recent cruise we noted a disturbing number 'temporarily' out of use; evidence of BW's budget being stretched?

The locks may, or may not, make life hard for the boater, but the canal itself is illuminated by a succession of small communities with interesting pasts. Sandbach stays a stubborn mile or more out of reach of the canaller, but you can savour the voyage around its outskirts and intermittent views of the tower of its parish church. At ETTILY HEATH the quadrupled, electrified tracks of the Crewe to Manchester railway cross the canal at the site of a transhipment basin provided to facilitate traffic with the Potteries. Hereabouts the canal, concrete-banked and steel-piled, tends to be deeper than is normal on account of subsidence caused by salt-mining in the past. The River Wheelock rises in the vicinity of Little Moreton Hall and gives its name to a former wharfingering community situated where the Crewe-Sandbach road crossed the canal. MALKIN'S BANK was home to the families of boatmen engaged in comparatively short-haul traffics connected with the salt and chemical industries. They lived cheek-by-jowl with employees at the huge Brunner-Mond sodium carbonate works which is now buried beneath the greens and fairways of Malkins Bank golf course. New housing has changed the atmosphere somewhat. Between locks 62 and 63, a side bridge carries the towpath over an old arm (now used by a boatbuilder) which once went into the chemical works.

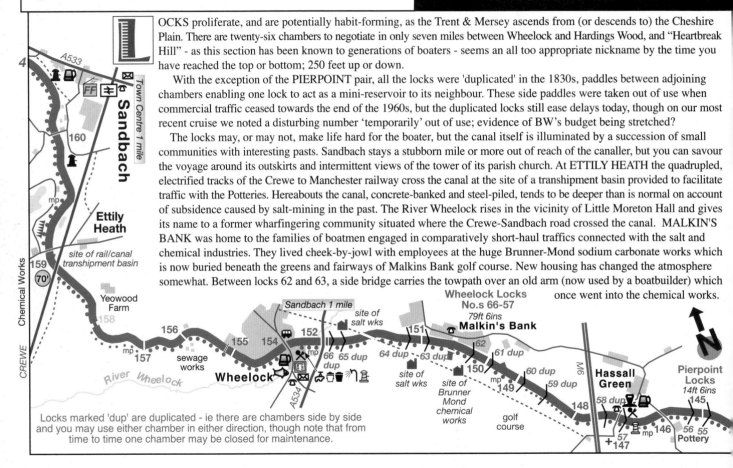

Locks marked 'dup' are duplicated - ie there are chambers side by side and you may use either chamber in either direction, though note that from time to time one chamber may be closed for maintenance.

Heartbreak Hill

65

NE hardly knows where to begin describing this richly rewarding length of the Trent & Mersey Canal as it makes its purposeful way through the long line of 'Cheshire Locks'. All the locks were duplicated under the direction of Thomas Telford in the 1830s, though one or two have since been singled. Most peculiar of all, perhaps, was the rebuilding of one of the Thurlwood Locks in 1958. Subsidence from the adjacent salt works had brought Lock 53 to the brink of collapse, and so a new chamber was designed in the form of a steel tank supported by a series of piers which could be raised should further subsidence occur. Entry to the chamber was through guillotine gates. In practice the steel lock took longer to operate and was mistrusted by boatmen. It had been out of use for many years before demolition in 1987.

Another structure of significance was lost to the canalscape at RODE HEATH where a large warehouse with arched loading bay stood beside the waterway until being controversially demolished in 1981. Hearing that the mill, a local landmark, was to be demolished, the Trent & Mersey

Canal Society successfully applied for the building to be given listed status. In response the mill's owners took the matter up with their local MP who managed to have protected status overturned. "After further consideration," quoted the DoE "we came to the conclusion that the building was not as interesting as at first thought."

LAWTON 'TREBLE' LOCKS are Telford's work and replaced a Brindley staircase which was both time consuming and wasteful of water. Beyond Church Locks there is a brief respite from the locks and the pleasant site of Lawton church at the edge of woods surrounding Lawton Hall. Throughout this length the countryside dips and sweeps away from the canal in folds and creases like a carelessly discarded garment, revealing lush pastures interrupted by pockets of woodland through which footpaths beckon enticingly. Mow Cop (pronounced to rhyme with 'cow') overlooks this delightful landscape from its high ridge, an appropriate platform for the sober, yet lofty ambitions of the Primitive Methodists

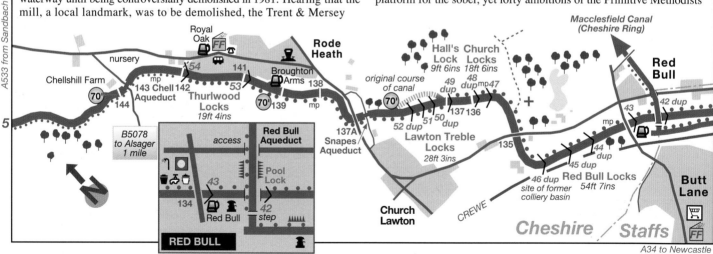

who held their first open air meeting on its summit in 1807. The castellated ruin, typical of 18th century romantic landscaping, is known as Wilbraham's Folly.

RED BULL LOCKS - once individually known as Townfield, Kent's and Yewtree in order of ascent - are probably the most visually satisfying on the whole of 'Heartbreak Hill'. All the elements are there by happy accident: a long, low stone wall separating the towpath from fields; the sweeping symmetries of the paired chambers masked from the railway by a high bank of beech trees; and an old whitewashed warehouse, once used for the storage of perishable goods, is now a facility centre for boaters.

POOL LOCK AQUEDUCT seems weighed down by the responsibility of carrying the Macclesfield Canal over the Trent & Mersey. It's not an elegant work of engineering, but it's stood here for 150 years and is no doubt good for a few more. Neither is the upper canal technically the 'Macclesfield', because it was the T&M themselves who built the Hall Green Branch, the Macclesfield Canal proper beginning at Hall Green stop lock one mile to the north beyond a second bridge, the Red Bull Aqueduct, which carries the canal over the A50 trunk road. The Macclesfield Canal is part of the popular "Cheshire Ring" canal circuit featured in another Pearson's Canal Companion and also recognised as a long distance footpath in its own right. Eastbound travellers along the Trent & Mersey, mystified by the Macclesfield's motive for crossing the T&M at this point, should turn to Map 7 for the exciting denouement.

Rode Heath & Thurlwood   *(Map 6)*
Two pubs vie for your custom: the BROUGHTON ARMS (Tel: 01270 765202), canalside by Bridge 139, and the ROYAL OAK (Tel: 01270 875670), reached from Bridge 142. Both are popular with boaters. Shops include a Chinese takeaway (Tel: 01270 873391), off licence and village store/post office. Buses run to The Potteries - Tel: 0870 608 2 608.

Red Bull & Butt Lane   *(Map 6)*
The RED BULL (Tel: 01270 782600) overlooks Lock 43. It is a cosy and welcoming pub whose beer comes from Robinsons of Stockport. Bar meals are usually available. Reginald Mitchell, designer of the Spitfire fighter aeroplane, was born nearby.

Kidsgrove   *(Map 7)*
A former colliery town on the wrong side of Harecastle Hill to qualify as a member of that exclusive hell fire club known as The Potteries. Its initially foreboding air thaws on closer acquaintance. A path leads up from the tunnel mouth to St Thomas's, "the bargee's church", and there are signposted ways through nearby "Kidswood". James Brindley is buried at Newchapel, a couple of miles to the east.

Eating & Drinking
There are several pubs adjacent to the canal, perennially the most interesting being the BLUE BELL (Tel: 01782 774052) overlooking Lock 41, which often wins awards for its wide choice of real ales.

Shopping
A large TESCO is conveniently reached from Lock 41, but Kiddy's more modest retailers are its strongpoint. Their shops may look dour from the street, but over the counter the natives are at their most vital. Surprisingly, the heart of the town lies not along the main thoroughfare, but on and around Market Street to the north. Here you will find a SOMERFIELD supermarket, butchers, bakers and a launderette. Make it your business to find BRENDA'S where you can watch oatcakes and pikelets, those twin bastions of North Staffordshire gastronomy, being freshly made on the griddle, and have your oatcakes crammed with a choice of fillings. Calor gas and solid fuel are obtainable by Bridge 132.

BUSES - Frequent services to Hanley and throughout the area. Tel: 0870 608 2 608. TRAINS - hourly services to/from Longport and Stoke - useful for towpath/tunnel top walkers and/or claustrophobics Tel: 08457 484950. TAXIS - Tel: 01782 775775.

Longport   *(Map 7)*
All the 'ports' - Long, Middle, West and New - lie down in the valley beside the canal and the origin of their names is obvious, forming as they do, a necklace of wharfingering communities where the import and export of cargoes of The Potteries were handled. Longport, lying as it does on an incredibly busy link road with the A500, makes few concessions in appearance. Lorries thunder through leaving a tidemark halfway up the fronts of shops where merchandising and point of sale are alien jargon.

BUSES - frequent services up the hill to Burslem - Tel: 0870 608 2 608. TRAINS - as per Kidsgrove.

T HARDINGS WOOD the Macclesfield Canal makes a junction with the Trent & Mersey. For eastbound travellers the mysteries of Map 6 are enlightened. If, on the other hand, you have just emerged, still blinking, from Harecastle Tunnel, you may be baffled to find a canal, destined for the north, making its exit to the south. All will be revealed on Map 6.

Taking a boat through Harecastle Tunnel is one of the great inland waterway adventures. There is a tunnel keeper at either end responsible for controlling passage through the narrow bore. You may be delayed waiting for oncoming boats to clear the tunnel before the keeper gives you, and perhaps others going your way, instructions to enter. Gingerly you penetrate the gloom beyond the portal. Gradually all sense of light is lost. Nostalgically you look over your shoulder at the retreating half-moon of daylight. Suddenly, with a shuddering clang, the doors at the southern end close and the fume extractor fans begin to suck with a muted roar. For the next three-quarters of an hour you are buried deep beneath Harecastle Hill: with one small niggle at the back of your mind,

will you or won't you come face to face with the 'Kidsgrove Bogart'?

The original tunnel through Harecastle Hill was designed by James Brindley. It took eleven years to build, was one and three-quarter miles long, and opened in 1777, five years after Brindley's death. A series of connecting tunnels led off the main bore to adjacent coal faces beneath Golden Hill, intersecting with several underground springs which provided additional water supplies to the summit level. A curious feature of this seepage occurs to this day, in that the water either side of the tunnel is tinted a peculiar orange shade by minute particles of ironstone rock.

For fifty years, teams of 'leggers' propelled boats through Brindley's towpathless tunnel, lying on their backs at right angles to the boat and literally 'walking' from one end to another, a feat which took two to three hours depending on the amount of alcohol consumed beforehand. Not surprisingly Harecastle became a serious traffic bottleneck. Reluctantly, being well aware of the costs and difficulties involved, the canal company commissioned a second bore with Thomas Telford as consultant engineer. Some idea of the advances in technology gained in the interim can be gauged from the fact that the new tunnel, equipped with a towpath, was completed in less than three years, opening in 1827.

Until the early years of the 20th century, the two tunnels were used in unison: Brindley's taking southbound boats, Telford's north. In 1914 electric tugs began to haul strings of boats through Telford's tunnel and Brindley's, now riddled with subsidence, was abandoned. The tugs were curious machines, unique on our waterways. They dragged

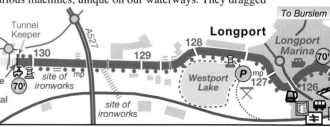

Harecastle tunnel timetable - see page 95

To A500

themselves along a steel cable laid on the canal bed, collecting power through a tram-like pole from an overhead cable. They successfully solved Harecastle's traffic flow problems into the 1950s, by which time the number of boats using the tunnel had diminished so as to render them unviable. In 1954 forced ventilation was introduced, enabling powered boats to pass through, a system still in use today. Further subsidence caused closure of the tunnel between 1973-77, but much money has been spent on its rehabilitation and it is now in excellent condition.

Refurbishment of the tunnel involved removal of the towpath, so walkers are faced with the option of catching a local train between Kidsgrove and Longport, or following the old boathorse route across the top, encountering the arcane, unvisited landscape of Harecastle Hill which Brindley and Telford must have been familiar with in their time. It seems little changed, and the chattering magpies which keep you company may quite possibly be re-incarnated navvies.

Nearing the hilltop, the lane becomes more potholed, bounded with rough pasture grazed by unkempt ponies, whilst airshafts trace the tunnel's subterranean passage, reminding you that there is a canal down there somewhere. An abattoir and traveller's camp intervene, whilst there are breathtaking views encompassing Jodrell Bank, the Wedgwood monument and the exciting urban panorama of the Potteries. In fact, all things considered, this is an adventure every bit as exciting as the boater's rite of passage underground.

Between Harecastle's southern portal and LONGPORT, the canal runs along its 408ft summit at the foot of a ridge supporting Tunstall, northernmost of the six Potteries towns. Industry once thronged the cut, but there

Longport Potbank

is an air of desolation here now. From Bridge 129 to 130 the vast Ravensdale ironworks framed the canal, as massive in its heyday as Shelton Bar, three miles to the south. Today, though, no trace remains at all. Indeed the only action is provided by cars and lorries thundering across the Tunstall by-pass, completed late in 1998. Nevertheless, for the industrial archaeologist the adrenalin will be flowing. Look out for Copp Lane canal cottages by Bridge 129, the ruined edge of the side bridge which spanned the ironworks arm, and the stubs of old basins where the gasworks stood by Bridge 128.

When Potteries folk lack the fiscal means to reach Rhyl or Blackpool, they come down for the day to Westport Lake where they can indulge in an ice cream cone and promenade the circumference of the lake, reopened after its landscaping by no less a personality than the former Prime Minister, Edward Heath. Good moorings are available here usually with the sense of security engendered by the proximity of fellow boaters. In the vicinity of LONGPORT some of the traditional aspects of North Staffordshire make their presence felt. A fine example of the once ubiquitous bottle kiln looms over the canal by a martial arts gym, whilst, another lies tucked away at the back of Middleport Pottery, where a couple of old cranes hang over the water's edge as if the arrival of the next narrowboat laden with felspar or flint is imminent. Longport Wharf itself remains intact, a typical canalside depot where consignments would be collected and delivered by road transport.

THE Trent & Mersey Canal plunges through the heart of the manufacturing district it was built primarily to serve - a heart, however, repeatedly broken as the age of coal gave way to the age of the computer. Until 1978 the canal penetrated the torrid core of Shelton Bar steelworks, scene of H. G. Wells' terrifying short story, *The Cone*, in which the steelmaster murders his wife's would-be lover by pushing him into a furnace. For a couple of decades thereafter only a rolling mill remained in use, though canal travellers were required to pass through the gloom of two overhanging fabrication sheds. In 2000 the plant closed, and had been totally obliterated by the time we researched this edition: no longer will you wave at the shunting engine drivers; no longer will the steelworkers cross the canal on their way back to Burslem at the end of a shift. In time some new development will rise from the rubble, sleek and shimmering and probably soul-less in the extreme.

The derelict acres left behind after demolition of the blast furnaces became the site of the 1986 National Garden Festival, subsequently developed into the Festival Park, a ubiquitous mix of leisure, retail and commercial facilities. Such transformations are not without irony. Centrepiece of Festival Park is an hotel converted from Josiah Wedgwood's original Etruria Hall built on a green-field site contemporary with the canal. During the 19th century the steelworks had encroached on the mansion, gradually engulfing its landscaped grounds. So, in a way, the developments of the 1980s returned the neighbourhood to its origins. Anyone familiar with the canal prior to the shutdown of Shelton Bar, however, is bound to mourn the lost drama associated with navigation through the cacophonous and acrid plant.

Like many heavily industrialised regions, The Potteries have passed through a period of transition; though here, perhaps, the pace of change has been less relentless, and something of the old atmosphere is still tangible. From time to time you come upon examples of the area's most potent symbol, the bottle kiln. There was a time, before the Clean Air Act, when visitors could purchase postcards depicting The Potteries' skyline blackened by the combined emissions from serried ranks of these ovens.

For reasons never convincingly explained, Arnold Bennett - who is to The Potteries as Hardy to Wessex or Lawrence to Nottinghamshire - always referred to just 'Five Towns' in his prolific novels and short stories which portray the area around the turn of the last century. He wrote that the Five Towns could never be described adequately because Dante had lived too soon. Inferno or not, five towns or six, there was always, and still to some extent is, a proud independence and individualism about The Potteries which sets it apart in an island between the Midlands and the North. Notice how the local accent has more in common with Merseyside than Manchester: could this have something to do with the development of the Trent & Mersey and the associations it prospered?

Between MIDDLEPORT and ETRURIA the canal twists and turns frequently, following the contours of the valley of the Fowlea Brook. Near Bridge 125 stands the terracotta gabled end of the Anderton Boat Company's former premises, a well known carrier in the district whose boats were nicknamed 'knobsticks'. Nearby, on a site now occupied by modern housing, stood Newport Pottery, famous for its connections with Clarice Cliff, the celebrated creator of 'Bizarre' and other Art Deco ceramics and pottery designs.

By Bridge 123 an arm once led to Burslem Wharf, scene of the pantechnicon's immersion in Bennett's hilarious novel, *The Card*. The arm was abandoned in 1961 after a breach caused by subsidence, but there have been proposals that it could be reinstated for moorings and leisure use.

Nowadays call centres and superstore outlets border the canal, but here and there are clues to a more colourful past: a boat dock beneath a roving bridge and another bridge where the 'Loop line' railway once weaved its way from one Six Towns community to the next. A wooden, windlass-operated lift bridge frames entry to the Festival Park Marina where secure moorings are available for an overnight stop and the chance to indulge in all the spurious activities modern life offers: supermarkets, ski slopes, swimming pools with wave machines, ten pin bowling alleys, fast food outlets and multiplex cinemas.

The modern premises of the local *Sentinel* newspaper occupy the original site of Wedgwood's pottery before subsidence and pollution forced the company to move to Barlaston (Map 9). All that remains of the pottery is an enigmatic roundhouse, one of a pair which fronted the works.

ETRURIA JUNCTION has all the ingredients of a compelling canalscape and ought to claim a spot in most enthusiasts' "Alternative Seven Wonders of the Waterways" along with such acquired taste locations as Windmill End, Wigan Pier and Trent Falls. Much of Etruria's surviving charm emanates from the juxtaposition of the two top locks of the Stoke Five and the handsomely constructed and resonantly named Etruscan Bone Mill lying beside a small arm issuing from the tail of the second lock down. This now houses the Etruria Industrial Museum, the entrance to which is beside the Caldon Canal. Also of interest

is the old graving dock, an intriguing milepost to Uttoxeter, a statue of Brindley, and the proximity of the deep staircase locks at the start of the Caldon Canal, all good stuff for the diehard to get their teeth into. Etruria's busy basin lay on the outside of the sharp bend at the commencement of the Caldon Canal. It did not always deal solely in goods. In the 1840s, during a time of recession for the pottery trade, large numbers of emigrants began a long, life-changing journey

continued on page 21

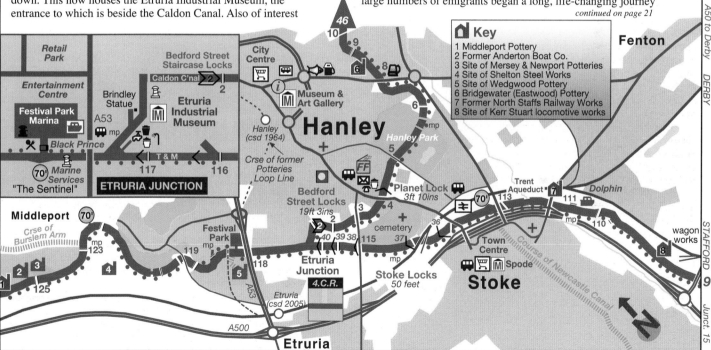

Key
1 Middleport Pottery
2 Former Anderton Boat Co.
3 Site of Mersey & Newport Potteries
4 Site of Shelton Steel Works
5 Site of Wedgwood Pottery
6 Bridgewater (Eastwood) Pottery
7 Former North Staffs Railway Works
8 Site of Kerr Stuart locomotive works

The Etruscan Bone Mill

Waiting for the Lock

Lock 38

FRANCES

continued from page 19

aboard narrowboats from this wharf, destined for Wisconsin in North America, where a township named Pottersville was established.

Southwards from Etruria, the Trent & Mersey negotiates STOKE LOCKS, a fascinating flight, brim-full of images jostling for your attention: a ruined flour mill by the third lock down; a cemetery providing a splash of green in a sea of otherwise grey industry; a pair of bottle ovens; a railway bridge carrying a siding into English China Clays' works (which receives this commodity in rail tankers now, whereas once it would have been brought round the coast from Cornwall to the Mersey and transhipped into narrowboats for the journey down to The Potteries) and the bottom lock in the flight, deep and concrete lined, a rebuilding dating from construction of the adjacent Queensway, itself again rebuilt in recent times to cope with ever increasing traffic levels.

By Bridge 113, the NEWCASTLE-UNDER-LYME Canal once diverged from the main line. Opened in 1798, it ran in a V shape for 4 miles to the nearby borough of that name which, curiously, already had a canal. The Sir Nigel Gresley Canal, a three mile private waterway unconnected with any other canals, had opened in 1775 to carry coal from outlying collieries belonging to the Gresley family into Newcastle itself. The Newcastle Junction Canal was subsequently built to link the two canals, but an inclined plane, planned to bridge the disparity in height between the two 'Newcastle' canals, was never constructed. Not surprisingly, all three canals were early casualties of the Railway Age. Stoke Boat Club used the first few hundred yards of the canal as moorings in the Sixties, but all trace of the entrance vanished with construction of the adjacent dual carriageway.

The canal crosses the tiny Trent, passing a small boatyard also offering, fishing, shooting and line-dancing facilities. Little evidence remains of Kerr Stuart's locomotive works where L. T. C. Rolt served an apprenticeship for three years from 1928. He writes vividly about his days in Stoke in *Landscape With Machines*, his first volume of autobiography. Happily a tradition of railway engineering continues in the shape of a modern wagon works. On the opposite bank of the canal, across the A500, is the site of Stoke City's former Victoria Ground, demolished when the club moved to their new Britannia Stadium just along the cut.

The Caldon Canal

Inland navigators, setting off from Etruria on the thirty mile trip to Uttoxeter, inferred by the milepost at the junction, are in for a disappointment. They can travel for seventeen miles to the remote wharf at Froghall, hidden deep in the woodlands of the Churnet Valley, but the canal onwards from that point to Uttoxeter itself was filled in and converted into a railway a century and a half ago. Nevertheless, the Caldon is one of the most delightful waterways in England, a thing of rare beauty, all the more enchanting because it is unfathomably under-utilised; though perhaps this only adds to its appeal in the eyes of connoisseurs.

From Etruria the Caldon Canal immediately declares its intentions, ascending a deep pair of staircase locks, followed by another single lock as it skirts Hanley, chief of the Six Towns. Dipping through an overbridge, it runs beside a stone wall over which peeps a typical Northern terrace. This simple throwback explains eloquently enough the inherent pathos of The Potteries: backyards with rainwater tubs and washing-lines; cobbled alleyways patrolled by stray dogs; net curtains blown softly by draughts unhampered by double-glazing. In another place, not far to the North, you would immediately think of Lowry or Coronation Street. But these are The Potteries, as warming, full of flavour, and insusceptible to the march of time as a Wrights steak & kidney pie.

Beyond Planet Lock the canal bisects HANLEY PARK, passing beneath a series of ornamental bridges. From a balcony embellished with terracotta, steps climb to a clock-towered pavilion from which you half expect Arnold Bennett characters to emerge at any moment.

Then follows a sad corridor of pottery works, for the most part derelict or demolished now, yet only a few years ago they were served by specially built craft carrying crockery from one department to another. This trade amounted to the final commercial use of a narrow canal anywhere in Britain. When we first covered this route in the mid 1980s the crockery boats worked out as far as Milton. Time was money and they didn't hang about. When you encountered one it was invariably accompanied by a tidal wave. As for the pottery factories, it is difficult to see any future other than demolition. And what then? More retail parks we'll be bound!

Continued on Map 46, page 84

Hanley (Map 8)

Arnold Bennett, his tongue perhaps not entirely in his cheek, called his 'Hanbridge' the Chicago of the Five Towns, which was his way of clarifying the confusing situation whereby it is Hanley that is the commercial heart of Stoke-on-Trent. Stoke is just one of the six communities, along with Tunstall, Burslem, Hanley itself, Longton and Fenton, that were merged to form Britain's fourteenth largest city in 1910. In any case the people of The Potteries have never been enamoured with the concept of belonging to an amorphous whole, preferring to shelter within the proudly individual characters of the six constituent towns. Hanley has suffered most from the pressures of the Consumer Age, and development has exorcised a good deal of the previously entrenched atmosphere of dignified northern provincialism. Heavens above, there is even a 'cultural quarter' now, something that would have Bennett choking on his Parisian cocktail had it occurred within his lifetime.

Eating & Drinking

PORTOFINO - Marsh Street South. Tel: 01782 209444. Stylish Italian restaurant.
MARMARIS - Percy Street. Tel: 01782 204499. Charming Turkish restaurant.
MINH'S - Albion Street. Tel: 01782 266410. Contemporary Oriental restaurant/bar.

Shopping

All facilities are available in the centre of Hanley which is about 20 minutes walk from the Trent & Mersey Canal at Etruria, but less distant from the Caldon Canal at Bridges 4 or 8. Frequent buses run from stops on Bridge 118. THE POTTERIES CENTRE houses all the usual chain stores, whilst the MARKET HALL also provides an outlet for local retailing. North Staffordshire delicacies include 'oatcakes' and 'pikelets'; whilst WRIGHTS have a number of shops and stalls selling their popular (albeit now Crewe-built) meat pies - head for Tontine Street and their coffee shop where you can sample their wares. Nearby is WEBBERLEYS bookshop and an interesting selection of local titles.

Numerous pottery works throughout the area have their own factory shops and visitor centres - a leaflet detailing these may be obtained from the Tourist Information Centre. Closer to the canal, there is a retail area at Festival Park dominated by a large Morrisons supermarket.

Things to Do

TOURIST INFORMATION CENTRE - Victoria Hall. Tel: 01782 236000 www.visitstoke.co.uk
POTTERIES MUSEUM & ART GALLERY - Bethesda Street, Hanley. Tel: 01782 232323. Open daily (afternoon only on Sunday), admission free. A superb museum which puts those of many larger cities to shame. The world's finest collection of Staffordshire ceramics, a section devoted to local man Reginald Mitchell's Spitfire fighter plane, and a rich collection of drawings, paintings and prints. Small corner celebrating Arnold Bennett.
ETRURIA INDUSTRIAL MUSEUM - canalside Bridge 116 (entrance beside the Caldon Canal). Admission charge. Tel: 01782 233144. Cafe and small shop. Restored potters mill of exceptional interest. The mill dates from 1857 and was built to grind animal bones for use in 'bone' china. Beam engine steamed monthly.
FESTIVAL PARK - Etruria. Attractions include: multi-screen cinema (Tel: 0871 224 4007); Waterworld swimming centre (Tel: 01782 205747); dry ski slope (Tel: 01782 204159); and ten pin bowling alley (Tel: 01782 289999).

Connections

BUSES - Excellent services throughout The Potteries. Tel: 0870 608 2 608. Vehicles display such evocative destination blinds as "Fegg Hayes" and "Talke Pits".

Stoke (Map 8)

Known as 'Knype' in Arnold Bennett's stories, Stoke was, and still is, the railhead for The Potteries. Here, his Five Towns characters waited for the old Loop Line trains to take them to 'Hanbridge' (Hanley), 'Bleakridge' (Cobridge) and 'Bursley' (Burslem). The station itself is an architectural gem, a sort of Jacobean mansion with platforms where you would might otherwise expect to find the croquet lawn. Across Winton Square, with its statue of Josiah Wedgwood, stands an equally imposing hotel. In the town itself the town hall and parish church make enduring architectural statements, but elsewhere the effect is largely lacklustre, apart from the old market hall's glazed and tiled frontage, all that survives from a fire on Cup Final day, 1982.

Things to Do

SPODE - Church Street. Tel: 01782 744011. visitor Centre, museum, factory shop and restaurant named after Spode's famous 'Blue Italian' range.

Connections

TRAINS - major railhead adjacent to Bridge 113. Tel: 08457 484950.
TAXIS - City Cabs. Tel: 01782 844444.

Barlaston (Map 9)

Suburbia has engulfed Barlaston, but a pub called the Plume of Feathers stands canalside and there's a useful row of shops west of Bridge 103 including pharmacy, Spar, butcher and newsagent. A Londis convenience store lies to the east of Bridge 103.

Things to Do

WEDGWOOD - adjacent Bridge 104. Visitor centre open daily throughout the year. Tel: 01782 282986. "Living museum, art gallery, gift shop, cinema, displays by skilled craftsmen."

EVERY city has its soft underbellys of suburbia, and Hem Heath is one of Stoke's; more so now that its colliery has been closed and razed to the ground. Following privatisation of the coal industry, there was a brave attempt to reopen the mine, though sadly this just postponed the inevitable. It's cheaper, it would appear, to buy coal from Australia nowadays than dig for it locally. Britannia Stadium has been Stoke City's home since 1997. Stanley Matthew's ashes are buried beneath the centre spot.

Blue brick abutments mark the course of the Trentham branch railway which, in its brief heyday, carried hordes of North Staffordshire day-trippers to the gardens of Trentham Hall. Trentham had been the seat of the Dukes of Sutherland, the most recent property having been completed in 1842 to the designs of Sir Charles Barry, architect of the Houses of Parliament. By all accounts it had been a most beautiful house set in the loveliest of landscaped parklands and Italian gardens. However, the Trent ran through these gorgeous grounds and, as the river grew more and more polluted by the combined effluents of The Potteries, life for the Duke, his household and visitors - which often included royalty - became less and less idyllic. Eventually the Duke was forced to quit Trentham for another of the family seats, and the hall was demolished just before the Great War. He left the grounds to the people of The Potteries and, as more sophisticated methods of sewage control were developed, Trentham Gardens became a celebrated resort for the residents of North Staffordshire. After a period in limbo, Trentham has been regenerated at considerable expense, and now once again features spectacular Italian Gardens . A tall monument commemorating the second Duke of Sutherland may be seen rising above woodlands to the west of Trentham Lock; as does one above the small coastal town of Golspie in Sutherland. Trentham Lock boasts a deep chamber with a pronounced undertow when filling. The foundations of its erstwhile keeper's cottage are readily apparent. Nearby stands the famous pottery works of Wedgwood. The company moved to Barlaston from their original site at Etruria in 1940.

The great Palladian facade of Barlaston Hall gazes benignly over the canal, a landmark case in the history of conservation. There were concerns that subsidence caused by mining at the former Hem Heath Colliery, which finally closed in the mid Nineties, might bring about its demolition, but its future was redeemed by the pioneering conservation group SAVE and, fully restored, it has become a private home once more. Barlaston is a popular overnight mooring point - details of its amenities appear on Page 22. At one time there was a busy boatbuilding yard here. A row of cottages occupied by its workforce - now highly desirable properties indeed - may be observed on the offside south of Bridge 103.

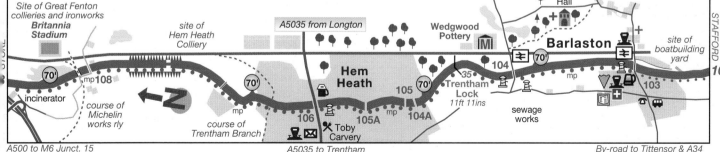

For details of facilities at Hem Heath and Trentham turn to page 25

MEAFORD Power Station is one of several along the Trent Valley demolished in recent years as the emphasis on the generation of electricity has shifted away from coal powered plants. There are four locks in the Meaford flight. Originally three of them were combined as a 'staircase'. Traces of the old course of the canal can clearly be seen to the west of the present layout. Meaford Locks form an attractive group (though in common with much of the Trent & Mersey's infrastructure and apparatus a pot or two of paint wouldn't go amiss) and are bordered by a country road with stone walling; one of the first signs that the Midlands are beginning to give way to the North. If you get into conversation with any locals it is disconcerting to hear them pronounce the place as 'Method'.

Making its way through the upper valley of the Trent, the canal encounters the market town of Stone, original headquarters of the Trent & Mersey Canal Company, which probably explains why the local foundry of Rangeley & Dixon won the contract to cast the T&M's distinctive mileposts. The town lost its role as the administrative centre for the canal when it was bought out by the North Staffordshire Railway in 1846, but retained an extensive dockyard for maintenance purposes. Nowadays the emphasis is obviously on leisure use, and there is still much to see as you chug through the four locks of the Stone flight. The second lock down, called Newcastle Road, is overlooked by the large convent school of St Dominic's which was designed by Joseph Hansom, the man who invented the Hansom cab. A boat horse tunnel leads underneath the road to a busy pound occupied by extensive linear moorings for private boats. Still quaintly signwritten, the former ale stores of Joule's Brewery border the canal before it widens by a fascinating spread of docks, covered and uncovered, wet and dry. These belong to the Canal Cruising Company, a pioneer of boating holidays on the canals, having been founded in 1948. It was here that L. T. C. Rolt's boat *Cressy*, of *Narrow Boat* immortality, met its end, being broken up and cremated after failing a survey in 1951. Yard Lock, located beside the boatyard, is the deepest of the flight. On the other side of the canal the town's former hospital - once a workhouse - has, rather ironically, been converted into prestige accommodation.

Star Lock is the bottom chamber in the flight. The pub from which it derived the name dates from the 16th century. An old warehouse on the offside below Bridge 93 has been converted into retirement flats, whilst several new buildings have been erected beside it in a pleasingly harmonious style. The canal company's offices stood alongside the towpath at this point, though there is no evidence of these now. They were demolished after the war, having been used for many years as a chocolate factory. Arguably the best moorings for access to the town are provided here, alongside a sportsground and children's play area.

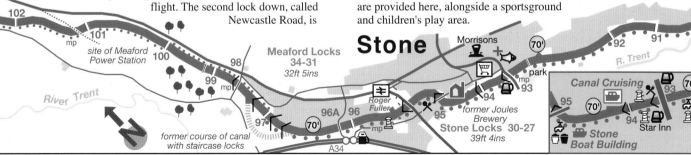

Stone (Map 10)

Stone is a lively market town of some twelve thousand souls. Conscious of their heritage, the local civic society have erected plaques on walls recalling that Peter de Wint, the landscape watercolourist, was born here; that the Duke of Cumberland came here to do battle; that the Star Inn has long attended to the thirst of passers-by; and that Henry Holland designed the bow-fronted Crown Inn in 1780. The demise of Joules remains Stone's great sadness. This proud independent had been brewing in the town since 1758 and, with the advent of the canal, and the possibilities of export it brought, their ales became fashionable in Europe and the Americas. Once they operated a pair of boats to bring in coal for firing the steam plant. As late as the 1950s their office retained the telephone number 'Stone 1'. But in 1970 they were absorbed into the Bass Charrington conglomerate and, hardly surprisingly, brewing ceased four years later; though the canalside ale stores remain intact. Bents, the town's other brewers, closed in the early 1960s, though bits of their brewery survive in industrial use and can be glimpsed by passing boaters above the Dutch gables of Stone's handsome railway station.

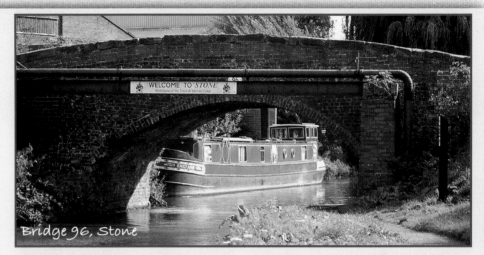

Bridge 96, Stone

Eating & Drinking

STAR INN - canalside Bridge 93. Quaint Banks's lockside pub serving a good range of food. Tel: 01785 813096.

SWAN INN - Lichfield Street (adjacent Bridge 93). Lively, CAMRA recommended town centre local offering replica Joules ales. Tel: 01785 815570.

LA DOLCE VITA - canalside Star Lock. Really nice lock-side Italian, substantial portions! Tel: 01785 817985.

PASTA DI PIAZZA - High Street. Tel: 01785 813214. Town centre alternative to above.

GRANVILLE'S - Granville Square. Tel: 01785 816658. Restaurant and music bar with the emphasis on jazz.

ISTANBUL - Lichfield Street. Tel: 01785 813334. Turkish restaurant.

HATTERS - Newcastle Road (adjacent Bridge 95). Well regarded restaurant with an imaginative menu. Tue-Sat evenings from 7pm. Tel: 01785 819292.

AL SHEIKH'S - Lichfield Street. Good Balti. Tel: 01785 819684.

THAI WELCOME - High Street. Tel: 01785 819000.

Shopping

Stone is a good shopping centre with the advantage of being so close to the canal that you can easily carry heavy carrier-bags back to the boat. Nice cakes from Hammersleys bakery on High Street. Somerfield and Morrisons supermarkets. Market on Tuesdays, Fridays & Saturdays. Farmers Market on the 1st Saturday of each month. Fine stoneware and bone china from DUNOON on High Street - Tel: 01785 818300.

Connections

BUSES - Services to/from Stafford and Hanley. Tel: 0870 608 2 608.

TRAINS - local services (currently provided by buses!) to/from Stoke and Stafford. Tel: 08457 484950.

Hem Heath & Trentham (Map 9)

Popular suburban stopping point with boaters. Handy shop and TOBY INNS steak bar - Tel: 01782 657316. About 15 minutes walk to the west, TRENTHAM GARDENS have benefitted from a multi-million pound makeover and attractions include a retail village, garden centre, woodland walks, 'monkey forest', boating lake and Italian gardens. Tel: 01782 646646 www.trentham.co.uk.

Joule's old ale stores, Stone

TAKING apparent pleasure in each other's company, canal and river, road and railway make their undemonstrative way through a shallow valley, skirting, but scarcely encountering, a succession of small settlements, barely in the category of villages. With no great dramas to catch the eye, the canal traveller is thrown back on his own resources. He can pass the time wrestling with the great conundrums of life or anticipate the slow drawing of a pint in the cool bars of the Greyhound at Burston or the Dog & Doublet at Sandon.

Aston Lock marks the half-way point of the Trent & Mersey's route from Preston Brook to Shardlow; names which mean nothing now but were once as well known as Spaghetti Junction and Watford Gap. One of the distinctive cast iron mileposts, originally made in Stone by Rangeley & Dixon, quotes 46 miles in either direction.

It is but a short stroll from Sandon Lock to the picturesque village of the same name. Sandon Hall, home of the Harrowbys, is a Victorian house in Jacobean style, well hidden from the world in rolling parkland. Above the woods peeps a slender urn-topped column commemorating William Pitt. Another Prime Minister, the assassinated Spencer Perceval, is remembered in a nearby shrine. Unfortunately the house and its grounds are only occasionally open to the public, but you can walk up the hill with the pheasants to the isolated church of All Saints to gain a panoramic view of the Trent Valley. Other points of interest in Sandon include the war memorial at the crossroads, the quaint 'arts & crafts' style village hall and matching pub, and the ornate former station house, notable for the *porte-cochere*, built to accommodate the carriage from Sandon Hall.

If you are undertaking a full circuit of the FOUR COUNTIES RING it is rewarding to contrast the character of the Trent & Mersey Canal with the Shropshire Union; barely ten miles away across country but a world away in style and atmosphere. Here the canal winds apparently arbitrarily beneath mellow brick accommodation bridges in a Georgian apothesis of grace, whilst the 'Shroppie', with its sturdy stone bridges, bold straights and Victorian sense of purpose, exudes an altogether different ambience.

Summary of Facilities
There are congenial country inns at Burston and Sandon: THE GREYHOUND (Tel: 01889 508263) and DOG & DOUBLET (Tel: 01889 508331) respectively. Both serve meals lunchtimes and evenings, the latter being open all day, nicely refurbished and offering accommodation to boot. Sandon also has a useful roadside stores.

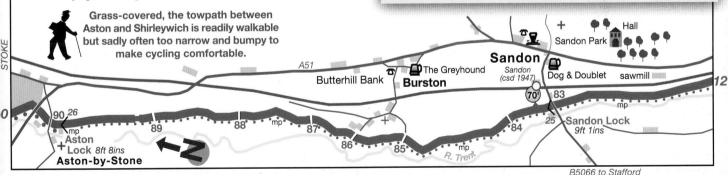

Grass-covered, the towpath between Aston and Shirleywich is readily walkable but sadly often too narrow and bumpy to make cycling comfortable.

Great Haywood

28

GIVEN the great beauty of the countryside, it is no coincidence that several wealthy and influential families put down grandiose roots here. Built of brick and stone for the benefit of Sandon's gentry, Bridge 82 echoes the high aesthetic values of the 18th century.

Any scar tissue wrought by the advent of the canal must have been healed by the time the railways arrived. The North Staffordshire Railway followed the course of the Trent & Mersey (which it was soon to acquire) down the valley to Colwich and became a main line of some importance as a through route between Manchester and London via The Potteries. Another line arrived in the landscape, was absorbed into the Great Northern Railway and became a far flung outpost of the LNER at the grouping of the railway companies in 1923. Passenger traffic was never significant - how could it be in these rural haunts? - but the milk of the Trent Valley's cows was creamy enough for the scheduling of a daily milk train to the capital. One activity in this otherwise rural area that the canal did help to prosper was the making of salt. The Trentside village of that name has associations with the trade going back to Medieval times; perhaps even Roman. But

at both Shirleywich and Weston brine pumping developed significantly in the 18th century because the canal was used to bring in coal to fuel evaporation and to carry away the finished product. Agriculture and industry combined to corner the market in salted beef for the Royal Navy, conveyed in barrels by narrow boat.

The towpath, indifferently maintained either side of Shirleywich and Pasturefields suddenly, but all too briefly, improves as part of a laudable local initiative. Between bridges 77 and 78 the canal runs alongside a rare example of an inland salt marsh.

Summary of Facilities

The HOLLYBUSH INN at Salt (Tel: 01889 508234) is highly regarded for its food. Alternatively you can sit on the village green at Weston outside the CAMRA recommended WOOLPACK (Tel: 01889 270238) after a hard day's boating, sample the SARACEN'S HEAD (Tel: 01889 270286) or stroll uphill to the restaurant facilties in WESTON HALL (Tel: 01889 271700).

With bicycles on board it's an easy detour to AMERTON WORKING FARM (Tel: 01889 271300) an entertaining mix of craft shops and farm animals with a narrow gauge railway to boot. Regular buses to Stafford and Uttoxeter - Tel: 0870 608 2 608. The village store at Weston is open daily.

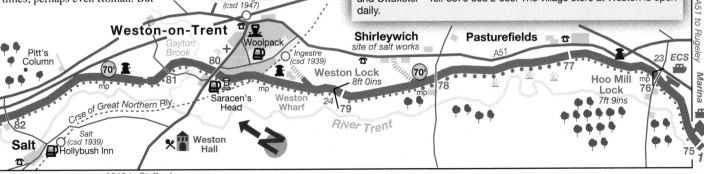

A518 from Uttoxeter
Amerton Working Farm 1 mile

Weston & Ingestre (csd 1947)

Weston-on-Trent

Gayton Brook

Woolpack

Pitt's Column

70'

81

80

Ingestre (csd 1939)

Saracen's Head

Weston Wharf

Weston Lock 8ft 0ins

24 79

Shirleywich site of salt works

70'

78

A51

Pasturefields

77

Hoo Mill Lock 7ft 9ins

76

23 ECS

A51 to Rugeley

Haywood Marina

Crse of Great Northern Rly

82

Salt

Salt (csd 1939)

Hollybush Inn

Weston Hall

River Trent

75 13

A518 to Stafford

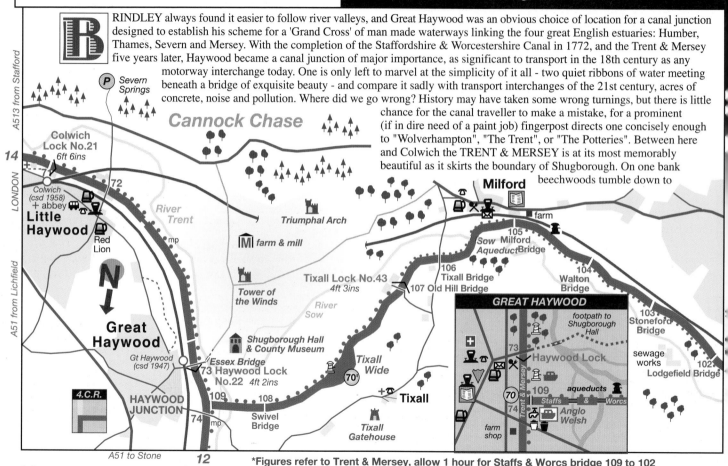

BRINDLEY always found it easier to follow river valleys, and Great Haywood was an obvious choice of location for a canal junction designed to establish his scheme for a 'Grand Cross' of man made waterways linking the four great English estuaries: Humber, Thames, Severn and Mersey. With the completion of the Staffordshire & Worcestershire Canal in 1772, and the Trent & Mersey five years later, Haywood became a canal junction of major importance, as significant to transport in the 18th century as any motorway interchange today. One is only left to marvel at the simplicity of it all - two quiet ribbons of water meeting beneath a bridge of exquisite beauty - and compare it sadly with transport interchanges of the 21st century, acres of concrete, noise and pollution. Where did we go wrong? History may have taken some wrong turnings, but there is little chance for the canal traveller to make a mistake, for a prominent (if in dire need of a paint job) fingerpost directs one concisely enough to "Wolverhampton", "The Trent", or "The Potteries". Between here and Colwich the TRENT & MERSEY is at its most memorably beautiful as it skirts the boundary of Shugborough. On one bank beechwoods tumble down to

*Figures refer to Trent & Mersey, allow 1 hour for Staffs & Worcs bridge 109 to 102

30

the water's edge. On the other, across the Trent, there are glimpses of the curious statues, antiquities and follies which pepper the grounds of this famous home of the Anson family. Colwich Lock lies in an attractive setting between the village church, a picturesque farm, and a bend in the river. From Bridge 72 you can take an idyllic walk to Severn Springs, a wonderful springboard for exploring Cannock Chase.

The Staffordshire & Worcestershire Canal

Through the arch of Bridge 109 - an 18th century fusion of functional engineering and enduring loveliness - the Staffordshire & Worcestershire Canal commences its 46 mile journey down to the Severn at Stourport. Two aqueducts carry it across the Trent and a millstream. A couple of miles further on it crosses the Sow. Between these river crossings the canal suddenly casts off its inhibitions and widens into a broad lake of quite un-canal-like proportions, bordered by thick reedbeds inhabited by a gorgeous array of wildfowl. Boaters will find their craft looping the loop out of sheer exuberance. This is Tixall Wide or Broadwater and there are two theories for its surprising existence. Some maintain that the canal was widened into an artificial lake to placate the owner of Tixall Hall. Others that the expanse of water predates the canal, that it was naturally formed, and that Izaak Walton learnt to fish here. Whichever explanation suits you, don't miss the extraordinary Elizabethan gatehouse which overlooks the Wide. The hall itself, where Mary Queen of Scots was imprisoned for a fortnight in 1586, was demolished long ago. The gatehouse is let for holidays by the Landmark Trust - Tel: 01628 825925.

West of Tixall's solitary lock the canal meanders enchantingly through the valley of the Sow. A plethora of trees adds lustre to the landscape. The river is crossed by way of a typical low-slung Brindley masonry aqueduct. Bridge 105 is a handsome turnover affair from which there is access under the railway to the village of Milford. Between here and Baswich the canal runs through fields between the river and the railway whose southbound trains are quickly gobbled up by the decorated portal of Shugborough Tunnel. Those of a railway bent may be intrigued to learn that Francis William Webb, the great locomotive engineer of the London & North Western Railway, hailed from Tixall, where his father was Rector for over half a century.

The Haywoods   (Map 13)

The villages of Great and Little Haywood are separated by the long, high brick wall of the Shugborough estate. Dormitory housing has inevitably expanded both populations, but the centres remain peaceful and largely unspoilt; especially so in the charming lane leading from Great Haywood, under the railway and over the canal, to the Essex Bridge, one of the finest examples of a packhorse bridge imaginable. Tolkien convalesced in Great Haywood after catching trench fever during the Battle of the Somme, and it is thinly disguised as 'Tavrobel' in *The Tale of The Sun and The Moon*.

Eating & Drinking
LOCK HOUSE - adjacent Haywood Lock. Tel: 01889 881294. Popular tea rooms and licensed restaurant. A pair of pubs in either village.

Shopping
Little Haywood has a post office stores (with cashpoint) and a newsagent. Great Haywood has two general stores (one with a butcher's counter), a pharmacy, post office, and a farm shop alongside the junction.

Things to Do
SHUGBOROUGH - access via Haywood Lock and Essex Bridge. Open daily April to December. Admission charge. Attractions include mansion, county museum, working farm, brewery, watermill, gardens, National Trust shop and cafeteria. A visit to the farm can be particularly recommended for families. Special events and a regular point of departure for hot air balloons.Tel:01889 881388 *www.shugborough.org.uk*

Connections
BUSES - Arriva service 825 operates half-hourly Mon-Sat (bi-hourly Sun) between Stafford and Lichfield via Rugeley. Tel: 0870 608 2 608.

Milford   (Map 13)

A motorist's gateway to Shugborough and The Chase unlikely to hold too much attraction for canal travellers. Throughout the summer its 'village green' is covered with parked cars. Facilities, however, include a steak bar, Britain's most long-lived WIMPY fast food outlet, post office store, newsagent and farm shop. Access from either Bridge 105 or 106. On Brocton Road MILFORD'S (Tel: 01785 662896) is a busy cafe celebrated for its cooked breakfasts and fish & chips.

THE river's slow influence pervades the canal, and the pair wander across the landscape like indolent lovers on a long afternoon, chaperoned at a discreet distance by the recumbent mass of The Chase. Several big houses were built by prosperous landowners in this enchanting countryside. The stuccoed facade of Bishton Hall overlooks the canal. Nowadays it is a prep school with an idyllic cricket ground shaded by ancient chestnut trees bordering the water. Another mansion, Wolseley Hall, stood opposite on the far bank of the river. It was demolished long ago, but the grounds have been incorporated into the Staffordshire Wildlife Trust's Wolseley Centre. Wolseley Bridge has graced the Trent here since 1800. It was designed by John Rennie, best known in canal circles for his work on the Kennet & Avon.

The towpath plays host to a pair of walking routes: the Staffordshire Way (Rudyard to Kinver) and Millennium Way (Newport to Burton-on-Trent). RUGELEY usually gets a bad press from guidebooks, but we have always had a soft spot for this down to earth little town, once home to the notorious

Victorian poisoner, William Palmer and also remembered as the scene, in 1839, of the canal murder of Christina Collins. In years gone by Rugeley was the site of a malodorous tannery (where flats have been built at Bridge 66) but it is the power station which dominates now, being opened here in the Sixties to take advantage of coal mined on the spot; though the colliery has closed and nowadays coal is brought in by train from far and wide - often having originated beyond these shores.

At Brindley Bank the canal suddenly stops running parallel with the Trent and turns sharply to cross it, as though Brindley had been screwing up his courage to bridge the river. Once there was a transhipment wharf here where flint was swapped between canal and river vessels for the short run down to Colton Mill by Trent Valley railway station. A handsome pumping station overlooks this crossing of water over water, though the aqueduct itself is of little aesthetic appeal. By Bridge 68 a short, reedy arm adjacent to the railway provides a useful turning point for lengthy craft. This may have been used as a transhipment basin in the fledgling days of the railway, perhaps for the conveyance of building materials.

CREWE & STOKE

site of trans-shipment basin

70'

68

69
mp

Trent Aqueduct

River Trent

Bishton Hall School

Pumping Station

Trent Valley

industrial estate

mp

power station

business park

mp

64

65

60'

Colwich

A51

70

Wolseley Centre

Garden Centre

67

Aldi

66

Morrisons

Rugeley

13

mp

Shimla Palace Antiques

Wolseley

A513

park

Town

Lichfield

WALSALL

Rugeley (Map 14)

A former mining town well versed in the vicissitudes of existence following the abandonment of the local pit in 1990. Scots accents are often to be heard, immigrants who came to work in the mine and remained washed-up by its callous closure. It's difficult to escape the impression that life here is lived on the cheap - though not without a certain deadpan dignity. Here in the tight-knit streets, and on the old Coal Board estates, one finds thrift and graft and a perverse civic pride, whilst a consoling beauty is to be found up on the nearby Chase.

Eating & Drinking
GEORGE & BERTIES - Albion Street. An unusual cafe with a central bar around which customers sit perched on high stools as if this were somewhere in Belgium. Tel: 01889 577071.
TERRAZZA - Italian restaurant housed in old chapel on Lichfield Street. Tel: 01889 570630.
INFINITY - Market Square. Tel: 01889 576727. Chinese buffet restaurant and take-away.

Shopping
Despite appearances, shopping in Rugeley can be fun. Moor north of Bridge 66 for easiest access to nearby town centre. Morrisons and Aldi supermarkets nearby. Market on Tue, Thur-Sat.

Connections
BUSES - services throughout the Trent Valley and Cannock Chase. Arriva service 825 links Rugeley with Stafford and Lichfield and is thus ideal for towpath walks. boaters with time to spare should take the Green Bus to Cannock, a magical mystery tour up and over The Chase. Tel: 0870 608 2 608.
TRAINS - sparse weekday service along Trent Valley (some provided by buses!) but more frequent from Town or Trent Valley stations to Stafford and Birmingham. Tel: 08457 484950.

Wolseley (Map 14)

Wolseley has a craft centre, antiques showroom, art gallery and garden centre (with cafe/restaurant) all accessible from Bridge 70.

Eating & Drinking
WOLSELEY ARMS - Tel: 01889 575133. The meeting place for the canal's promoters.
SHIMLA PALACE - Tel: 01889 881325. Indian restaurant, eat in or takeaway.
THE WOLSELEY CENTRE - Tel: 01889 880100. Staffordshire Wildlife Trust headquarters set in revitalised garden park.

Handsacre (Map 15)

The High Bridge spanning the Trent to the north of Bridge 58 is worth a sortie ashore; its graceful single cast-iron arch made at Coalbrookdale in 1830. THE CROWN (Tel: 01543 490239) is a congenial Bass local where the repartee is apt to be as frothy as your pint. Frequent queues testify to the quality of the fish & chips from MICHAEL'S just up the road and there's a quaint cafe called SELWOOD HOUSE (Tel: 01543 490480) which does "the best breakfasts in Staffordshire" from 7am - accommodation is also available which may be of interest to towpath walkers.

Armitage (Map 15)

Offside moorings provide access via an alleyway to a number of shops on the main road.
THE PLUM PUDDING BRASSERIE - canalside Bridge 61A. Tel: 01543 490330. Winner of 'A Taste of Staffordshire' award. Accommodation also available.
SPODE COTTAGE - across road from above. Tel: 01543 490353. Bar/restaurant.
ASH TREE - canalside Bridge 62. Tel: 01889 578314. 'Two for One'.

Alrewas (Map 16)

A fundamentally pretty village not entirely compromised by the grafting on of new housing. Pronounced 'Ol-re-wuss', the name is derived from the presence of alder trees in the vicinity which were used in basket making.

Eating & Drinking
THE CROWN - Post Office Road. Tel: 01283 790328. *Good Beer Guide* recommended.
WILLIAM IV - near Bridge 46. Tel: 01283 790206.
THE OLD BOAT - beside Bagnall Lock. Tel: 01283 791468.
ALREWAS CANTONESE - Tel: 01283 790027.
ALREWAS FRYER - Tel: 01283 790432. Fish & chips.

Shopping
BARKERS food emporium, which dated back to 1924, has sadly bit the dust, but the excellent COATES butcher's shop continues to thrive, specialising in locally reared meats, boasting a wide choice of game, and also dealing in excellent pies, cheese and flour. Also: an off licence, chemist, newsagent and Co-op store (with cash machine) open late Mon-Sat.

Things to Do
NATIONAL MEMORIAL ARBORETUM - Croxton Road (approximately 1 mile south of Bridge 49A - beware busy roads). Tel: 01283 792333. Developing attraction incorporated in the new National Forest as a tribute to those affected by wars throughout the 20th century. Fifty thousand trees have been planted on a 150 acre site beside the River Tame. Two minute silence, reveille and last post enacted daily at 11am. Shop, and cafe/restaurant.

Connections
BUSES - Regular services to/from Burton and Lichfield (well worth considering as an excursion ashore). Tel: 0870 608 2 608.

WHILST by no means a length of canal likely to endear itself to connoisseurs of the picturesque, this stretch of the Trent & Mersey is never actually overwhelmed by industry, and there are a number of invigorating views over the Trent Valley or up on to the flanks of Cannock Chase.

The characteristic Trent & Mersey mileposts measure your progress, more relevant perhaps to the perspiring towpath walker than the languorous boater, laid-back on their tiller. They were put in place originally to facilitate the calculation of tolls, but at the outset of the Second World War, in common with most of Britain's road and railway signs, they were removed to befuddle invading Ayrans. Remarkably, following a commendable campaign by the Trent & Mersey Canal Society in the 1970s, they have all been returned to their rightful places. The originals bear the inscription 'R&D Stone 1819', the replicas cast to replace those which had 'disappeared' during the interim, are inscribed 'T&MCS 1977'.

Armitage and Shanks are synonymous with toilet plumbing. Their trade marks are emblazoned on public conveniences throughout the world. Once they were separate firms, merging in 1969, but the site alongside the canal at ARMITAGE dates back to 1817. Sanitaryware became a speciality in the 19th century under the management of Edward Johns - the origin of the Americanism "Going to the John". Today the factory, towering over a narrow stretch of canal spanned by the West Coast Main Line railway, is huge and convincingly

prosperous, and Armitage Shanks are a public limited company with a seemingly 'watertight' future.

Connections are apparent with another famous earthenware firm at Spode House and Hawkesyard Priory. Josiah Spode, a member of the North Staffordshire pottery family, left his house to a Dominican Order in 1893 and the monks proceeded to build a priory in the grounds, completing the work just prior to the First World War. The priory is now a day spa and retreat whilst the grounds have become a golf course.

Armitage's church is perched above a sandstone bluff by Bridge 61. Though much rebuilt by the Victorians, it retains its highly decorated Norman door. A path worth taking leads beneath the railway and over the Trent to the isolated settlement of Mavesyn Ridware which also has an interesting church. Occasionally, whether travelling on foot or afloat, you just feel the urge to turn your back on the canal.

Passing beneath the A513, the canal narrows and negotiates a rocky cutting. One-way working is the order of the day. This was formerly the site of Armitage (or "Plum Pudding") Tunnel, a dramatic unlined bore through the rock face. Subsidence, induced by coal mining, necessitated opening out of the tunnel, and concrete lining of the canal banks.

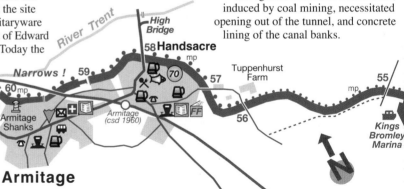

A bend in the canal south of Woodend Lock, and glimpses of the three spires of Lichfield Cathedral, tell you that you and the Trent & Mersey have travelled as far south as you are ever going to get in the canal's arc-like journey between Preston Brook and Shardlow. Ravenshaw Woods are a riot of rhododendron colour in early summer. The works by Bridge 54 was once the smelly "milk factory" referred to by L. T. C. Rolt in *Narrow Boat*.

FRADLEY JUNCTION'S fame far outweighs the sum of its parts. All that ever seems to change is the music emanating from the crowded interior of "The Swan". On hot summer days the junction is hugely popular with sightseers, but on winter afternoons it isn't difficult to imagine how it must have looked in the latter days of cargo carrying, as memorably described by Tom Foxon in his book of working boatman reminiscences, *Number One!*.

The Coventry Canal heads off in a southerly direction towards Fazeley and Tamworth - a route covered in our "South Midlands" and "Stourport Ring" Canal Companions. British Waterways' local manager and his staff occupy the neat former 'company' maintenance yard located between Keeper's and Junction locks. A canal shop and cafe are recent additions to this attractive scene. On the opposite bank private woodland masks Fradley Reservoir, which, in recent years, has been opened out as a visitor attraction. Between Fradley and Alrewas the canal crosses former common land and the flat nature of the adjoining fields engenders a distinct feeling of emptiness. The canal curves endearingly through the picturesque village of Alrewas, long ago a centre of basket weaving. Below Alrewas Lock the canal merges with the River Trent for a short distance before the river plunges unnervingly over a large weir. The towpath is carried over a mill stream, the main channel of the river, and a succession of reedy backwaters by an attractive series of metal footbridges.

Fradley Junction
THE SWAN - canalside, Fradley Junction. Tel: 01283 790330. This well known former boatmen's pub plays a leading role in the social life of Fradley Junction, being popular with boaters and motorists alike. Additionally, refreshments available from British Waterways' cafe (Tel: 01283 790236) and the Kingfisher Holiday Park - Tel: 01283 790407.
TAXIS - Alrewas Taxis. Tel: 01283 790391

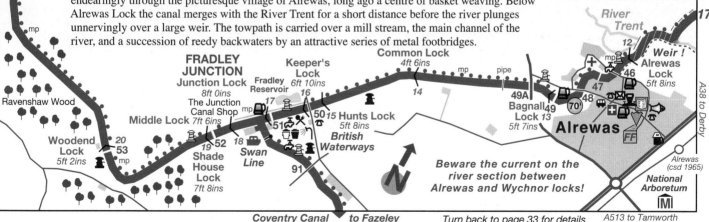

Turn back to page 33 for details of Alrewas and its facilities.

The Trent & Mersey near Alrewas

KEEPING company with the Roman's Ryknield Street, the canal traverses the broad, flat valley of the Trent; a landscape of gravel pits and distant villages backed by low-lying hills. Between Alrewas and WYCHNOR the canal suddenly assumes a quite different character as it negotiates a marshy, almost ethereal stretch of countryside, criss-crossed by drainage channels, or 'sitches', which thread their way through meadowlands to meet the Trent. It is a sudden, yet subtle, scene change. The domesticity of Alrewas village and the cacophony of the A38 are briefly forgotten, as the waterway puts you tantalisingly in touch with a past inhabited by eel-catchers, reed-cutters and sluice-keepers.

Wychnor was the scene of a tradition, similar to the more famous one at Dunmow in Essex, whereby any man who could swear not to have wished to exchange his wife for another woman, at any time during the first year of his marriage, was entitled to a flitch of bacon from the Lord of the Manor. It may - or may not - surprise you to learn that the flitch was never successfully claimed. Wychnor Church, reached from Bridge

45, dates back to the thirteenth century although the tower is a much later addition.

All along the A38 corridor business parks are burgeoning. Virgin Trains 'Voyager' fleet is maintained at the Central Rivers Depot. The massive distribution centre for Argos dominates the landscape unequivocally . Depressing to see, however, that it isn't linked to the railway, let alone the canal. BARTON TURNS wharves were provided for the villages of Barton and Walton, each a mile or so from the canal on opposite sides of the Trent. A large marina offers moorings and boating facilities to the north of Barton Turns. Fifteen minutes walk away, Barton-under-Needwood itself is a useful source of supplies and refreshment. When the bridge across the river to Walton was damaged by floods in the 1940s, it was replaced by a 'temporary' Bailey bridge - it is still in use!

Drakelow Power Station, a Trent Valley landmark since the 1950s, was demolished in 2006. TATENHILL LOCK lies in a deceptively remote setting. The former lock-keeper's house is now a private dwelling. A path runs from Bridge 35 between old gravel workings in the direction of the village of Tatenhill, tucked demurely away between folds of the Needwood Hills. The Forest of Needwood was once one of the largest royal hunting grounds; little woodland now remains, although trees are returning with the establishment of the new National Forest.

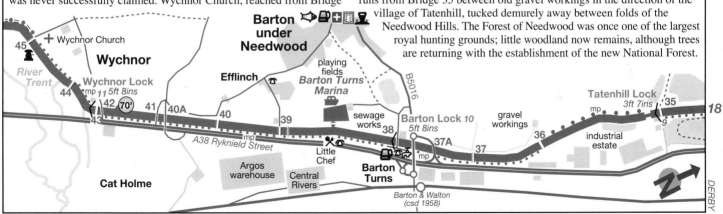

THE brewery town of Burton-on-Trent presides over the Trent & Mersey Canal's change of gauge: east of Dallow Lane the locks will be widebeam. When the canal opened in 1770, it brought a rapid decline in the use of the River Trent, which had itself been made navigable up to Burton at the beginning of the 18th century. To serve wharves established on the riverbank, however, a branch canal was built from Shobnall to Bond End. When the Birmingham & Derby Junction Railway was opened a drawbridge was provided to carry the line over this Bond End Canal. In 1846 a southbound train plunged into the canal because the bridge had been opened for the passage of a boat in the mistaken belief that no train was due!

Bridge 34 at BRANSTON is a popular mooring point for boaters attracted by the canalside pub. Beyond the towpath hedge the adjoining flooded-out gravel workings have been transformed into a 'water park'. Between Branston and Shobnall the canal runs at the foot of an escarpment marking the edge of what was once the Forest of Needwood. The half-timbered house on the hill is Sinai Park which belonged to the Benedictine monastery founded in the town in 1004. The main part of the abbey lay beside the river, but Sinai Park was used variously as a hunting lodge, summer house and blood-letting sanatorium.

It is at SHOBNALL that the canal traveller becomes most aware of Burton-on-Trent's stock in trade. West of the canal stands Marston's brewery, to the east the Coors Maltings. Visitors are quick to remark upon the aroma of hops in the vicinity, though locals are largely inured to the aromatic tang of the town. A common misapprehension is that Burton derives its excellence in brewing from Trent water. In fact the water used for brewing lies on beds of gypsum rock beneath the town and is pumped to the surface. The predominance of such stone made Burton a centre for the production of alabaster ornaments in the middle ages.

One of the once numerous branch railways, linking the main lines with Burton's breweries and other industries, paralleled the canal on its way through the town. Nowadays it's used as a public footpath and cycleway. In its heyday, Burton's 'internal' railway system was so dense that there were an astonishing thirty-two level crossings in the town. The railways captured the bulk of beer transport from the canal, but at the end of the 18th century large volumes of ale were being exported via Hull to northern Europe, the Baltic and Russia, and via Liverpool to India and South America.

Until the late 1970s the basin at HORNINGLOW was overlooked by a salt warehouse, part of which actually spanned the canal, so that boats heading east appeared to vanish into a 'tunnel'.

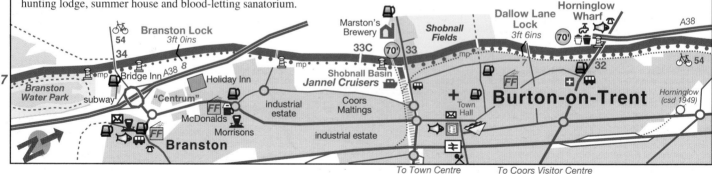

Barton under Needwood   *(Map 17)*

Mellifluously named but much enlarged village with good shopping facilities and several pubs approachable via footpath or B5016.
BARTON TURNS - Bridge 38. Tel: 01283 712142. Open daily noon to 11pm. Cosy canalside pub serving Marston's and guest ales. Homely menu of inexpensive food. Meals in the basket!

Branston   *(Map 18)*

Once a village, and the unlikely birthplace of a well known pickle relish, now a much-expanded suburb; hardly pretty, but useful for its facilities.
BRIDGE INN - canalside Bridge 34. Tel: 01283 564177. Former boatman's pub serving Marston's Pedigree along with a largely Italian inspired menu. Pleasant canalside garden.

Through the underpass, Branston also boasts a fish & chip shop, a Chinese take-away and two further pubs. Use this subway beneath the road interchange to reach the shops, five minutes walk from Bridge 34.

Burton on Trent   *(Map 18)*

With a courteous nod in the mellower directions of Tadcaster, Hook Norton and Southwold, this is the definitive brewery town, albeit one rendered increasingly anodyne as merger succeeds merger. At the turn of the century there were over twenty breweries in the town. Rationalisation has reduced this to just two mainstream concerns, Coors and Marstons, plus three micro-breweries. So "Beertown-on-Trent" still reverberates to its stock in trade, though for anyone who knew it prior to the contraction of the brewing industry and the closure of its quaint network of interconnecting railway lines, the place is an 'Indian Pale' shadow of its former self. The bulk of Burton's brewing infrastructure has been a regrettable casualty of Progress. Compare the realistic model in the Coors Visitor Centre with the present's ersatz reality, and you too will mourn the loss of so many maltings and brewing plants, quite literally 'gone for a Burton', as they used to say of downed pilots during World War II.

Eating & Drinking

THE ALBION - third of a mile to north of Shobnall Basin. A 'two for one' Marston's pub with a large garden. Tel: 01283 568197.
BILL BREWER - Centrum, Branston. 'Two for One' family pub. Tel: 01283 542321.
THE MILL HOUSE - canalside Bridge 29A, Map 28. All day family pub. Tel: 01283 535133.
BURTON BRIDGE INN - mile south of Horninglow Wharf. Worth the long trek to sample the town's doyen micro-brewery. Tel: 01283 536596.
COOPERS TAVERN - Cross Street. Tel: 01283 532551. Cosy treasure. Turn right off Station Street on your way into the town centre.
MYKONOS - Borough Road. (adjacent station). Tel: 01283 533178. Greek restaurant.
TASTE - Station Street. Tel: 01283 516859. English/European cuisine over the station bridge.
THE BREWERY TAP - Coors Visitor Centre, Horninglow. Tel: 01283 513757. Bar and restaurant.

Shopping

The town centre is 15-20 enervating minutes walk from the canal, though buses operate from both Horninglow and Shobnall basins. Closer at hand there are shops along the length of Waterloo Street easily reached from Dallow Lane and Shobnall. Market days Thur-Sat.
MORRISONS supermarket is nearest the canal (along with McDONALDS) at Branston.
MARSTON'S BREWERY SHOP lies a tempting 250 yards west of Bridge 33.

Things to Do

TOURIST INFORMATION - Coors Visitor Centre, Horninglow Street. Tel: 01283 508111.
COORS VISITOR CENTRE - Horninglow Street (10 mins walk from Horninglow Wharf) Tel: 0845 600 0598. Open daily, admission charge. Fascinating displays of the development of Burton brewing. Shire horse and rail and road transport exhibits. Good catering - ideal for lunch.
CLAYMILLS PUMPING STATION - 5 minutes walk from Bridge 29, Map 28. Open Thursday & Saturday for static viewing - special steaming days detectable by a pall of smoke over the surrounding countryside. Tel: 01283 509929. Four beam engines and five boilers in a Grade II listed sewage pumping station dating from 1885.

Connections

BUSES - local services throughout the Trent Valley. Tel: 0870 608 2 608.
TRAINS - half-hourly local service to/from Birmingham, Derby & Nottingham; bi-hourly Virgin 'inter-city' services. Tel: 08457 484950.
TAXIS - Station Taxis. Tel: 01283 532000.

Repton & Willington   *(Map 19)*

A useful watering hole with a trio of cosy pubs, Co-op store, delicatessen, pharmacy, post office, railway station and florist should you want to say "sorry" for shouting at her at the lock. But Willington's real significance lies in its proximity to the ancient settlement of Repton on the far bank of the Trent. Pinpointed by the slender spire of St Wystans, Repton is a worthwhile fifteen minute walk from the canal. The church is of Saxon origin, Repton having been the capital of Mercia in the 9th century until laid waste by marauding Danes. Nowadays the village is best known for its public school. Several good inns and a farmhouse tearoom offer refreshment.

EAST of Burton, the Trent & Mersey doesn't exactly flaunt its freshly acquired widebeam status. True, the bridge-holes are more buxom, but it is not until Stenson Lock is reached, that the true gauge of the canal manifests itself. Barge wide vessels traded upwards from Nottingham to Horninglow until the railways took a grip of the trade in beer; thereafter, even narrowboat traffic dwindled between Fradley and Shardlow. One of the last regular consignments was of cardboard for the manufacture of cigarette papers by Players at Nottingham.

Bridge 31 carries a link road occupying the trackbed of the North Staffordshire Railway's Burton to Tutbury branchline, haunt of a push & pull shuttle known as "The Jinnie". Beyond Stretton the course of the line has become a footpath and nature reserve. Rubber making is a lesser-known facet of the brewery town's economy, though the canalside Pirelli plant has shed much of its workforce in recent times.

Passing over the border between Staffordshire and Derbyshire, marked by an old mill race, the canal crosses the Dove upon a low-slung aqueduct designed by Brindley and refurbished in 2003. Beloved of Izaak Walton, the River Dove is virtually at journey's end here, being less than a mile from its lonely confluence with the Trent at Newton Solney; all a far cry from the glories of Dovedale and the Peak District. An adjacent road bridge, reputedly built by the monks of Burton Abbey, compensates for the aqueduct's plain appearance. On sultry summer days, in spite of dangerous whirlpools, local youths swim in this reach of the Dove.

An imposing Georgian wharf house overlooks Bridge 26 and the site of Egginton's old village wharf. Otherwise the canal is largely featureless as it makes its way through the Trent Valley, as if handcuffed by the portly escorts of a busy dual-carriageway and a main line railway. A pleasant ridge dominates the southern horizon, leading to the stiletto-fine spire of Repton church.

WILLINGTON, a commuter village dominated by a lugubriously derelict power station, sets its stall out to attract canal visitors. The site of an old rail/canal transhipment wharf has been landscaped and a car park provided for motorists - full of sleeping reps more often than not.

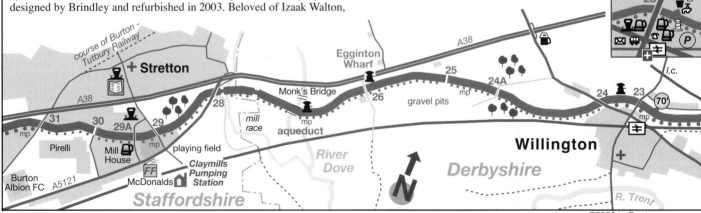

Turn to page 39 for summary of facilities at Willington & Repton

40

T was at Findern that 'the worst storm either of us had ever experienced, raging without pause for over three hours' overtook Tom and Angela Rolt aboard *Cressy* in 1939. A few days later an even greater storm erupted as Britain declared war on Germany.

Unlike Drakelow to the west, and Castle Donington to the east, the defunct power station at Willington has retained its cooling towers, mute testimony to a means of generating electricity now deemed as obsolete as the indigenous collieries which served such coal-fired enterprises.

When the railway was built, track ballast was sourced locally, by the simple expedient of digging it out of the ground. The holes thus formed filled with water and became amenities. An old signal box was purloined to act as a pavilion, and a boat provided from which to sit and fish or simply to sit and wonder. In its working days the power station was allowed to stuff these charming ponds with waste ash. But one between the railway and the canal has recently been revived and equipped with a pond-dipping platform,

making it a nice spot to have a picnic whilst pondering on the certain truth that today's cutting-edge technology is tomorrow's leisure opportunity. Talking of technology, Toyota's huge car plant lies just over the brow of a hill to the west of the canal, occupying the site of Derby's former municipal airport.

Between Stenson and Swarkestone the canal slinks furtively through fields given over to vegetable growing. The feeling that one is a long way from anywhere is misleading. Derby lies just over the rim of the northern horizon. Even closer is the busy A50 trunk road, which serves as a link between the M1 and M6 motorways. But then canals have a knack of conjuring a stimulating sense of isolation in the most unpromising of circumstances. Near Bridge 16, a moving little memorial commemorates the tragic death of a teenage girl in 1978.

The railway which parallels the canal most of the way between Stenson to Sawley lost its regular passenger services thirty years before Beeching reared his ugly head, though from time to time diverted passenger trains still use it at the weekends. Normally, only goods trains pass over its tracks now, and the romantic sounding wayside station called Castle Donington & Shardlow is as distant a memory as working boats on the canal.

Summary of Facilities
There are no shops at all within easy reach of this length of canal, but there are several places where you can eat and drink. By Bridge 21 a former canalside pub has been revitalised as an Indian restaurant called NADEE - Tel: 01283 701333. Stenson is a well known canal centre with barn-conversion pub called THE BUBBLE - Tel: 01283 703113. Teas and gifts from the lock house. Between bridges 17 and 18 RAGLEY BOAT STOP (Tel: 01332 703919) is a family pub converted from an old farm house. Customer moorings are provided on the opposite side to the towpath and water and electricity are laid on for boating patrons at the foot of a long lawn.

41

EVER more than half a mile away from the Trent, and often closer, the canal travels through mellow countryside, much of which is given over to market-gardening. Evidence of occupation by the Beaker People sixteen hundred years before the birth of Christ suggests that man's influence on Swarkestone goes a long way back. Swarkestone Bridge is of relatively modern origin, dating back only to the 12th century. It is generally regarded as the longest stone-built bridge in Britain. In 1347 the scale of tolls quoted charges of a ha'penny for a cask of sturgeons. In 1745 this was the furthest south that Bonnie Prince Charlie's army got in their attempt to capture the throne of England. Just twenty-five years later the Trent & Mersey was being dug, and soon afterwards Swarkestone became the site of a junction with the Derby Canal, including a branch down to the river which only survived until around 1800.

The Derby Canal, overlooked by nationalisation in 1947, was acrimoniously abandoned in 1964, though trade had ceased twenty years earlier. The company who owned the canal were well aware that more money could be made from property deals than from running a public waterway. The old junction house remains intact, used, like the one at Huddlesford on the Coventry Canal, by a local boat club. The Derby Canal's towpath has been resurfaced as part of National Cycle Route 6 and there are ambitious plans to restore at least part of the canal (which linked with the Erewash Canal at Sandiacre) to navigable standard.

By Weston Cliffs the canal glides through tumbling woodland. While construction of the canal was proceeding eastwards, a wharf was erected here for the transfer of goods from barge to riverboat. Later it was used for the transhipment of gypsum bound from Aston to King's Mills, whereupon, after being ground, the resultant plaster was despatched back up the canal for consignment via Swarkestone and the

Map labels

Course of Derby Canal & Derby Cycle Route

A50

Swarkestone Stop
S.B.C.
70'
15
14
mp
5
13
Cuttle Bridge
course of Derby & Ashby Railway
A50
Swarkestone Lock
10ft 11ins
A514
course of former link with Trent
Crewe & Harpur
The Stand
Swarkestone
20
6
12
mp
River Trent
6
Swarkestone Bridge
Sailing Club
N
Stanton by Bridge
70'
11
site of Military Railway depot
Tarasivka
course of Derby & Ashby Railway
viaduct
Weston Cliffs
viaduct
site of Bridging School
A514 to Swadlincote
Derby Cycle Route (Melbourne 1 mile)
10
former wharf
9
Weston-on-Trent
Cooper's Arms
Old Plough
Weston (csd 1930)
Weston Lock
10ft 11ins
4
mp
8
Weston Grange
mp
7
R. Trent
site of ferry
site of lock
King's Mills
Derbyshire
Leics.
2
By-road to Castle Donington
A5132 from Willington

Derby Canal to a building merchant in Derby. In these days of the ubiquitous lorry, the labour-intensiveness of previous eras of transport is astonishing.

During the Second World War this dreamy riparian landscape was rudely awakened by the construction of an army camp at Weston Cliffs. It was built to house the army's railway engineers who operated the Melbourne and Ashby line as a military railway during the Second World War. The army camp also provided accommodation for soldiers attached to a Bridging School opened across the river at King's Newton. As part of their training they built a now vanished suspension bridge across the river to facilitate access between the camp and the school. The enigmatic remains of a steam crane used by the bridge-makers remains by the handsome cast-iron railway viaduct which now carries Cycle Route 6 across the Trent near Bridge 11. The trackbed of that line has been imaginatively resurfaced to create a traffic-free link between Derby and the handsome old market town of Melbourne.

Hardly had the railway engineers marched away, before the camp was commandeered to house Ukrainian refugees. Several hundred arrived here to escape oppression in their homeland in 1944. Weston Rectory, visible on its low hilltop to the north of the canal, was used as a home for the centre's elderly residents, whilst parts of the camp were used by Ukrainian youth groups. A number of Ukrainian children were accommodated here following the Chernobyl nuclear disaster. The camp is known as Tarasivka and includes a tiny wooden chapel and a memorial to those who gave their lives for freedom in the Ukraine.

The lane from Bridge 8, by Weston Lock, provides easy access to Weston village in one direction. In the other it offers a peaceful walk down to the site of an old lock opposite King's Mills, a popular bathing spot until demolition of a weir in 1957 rendered such activities dangerous. Rummage in the undergrowth and you may discern the remains of the old lock. In the past there was a ferry here too, providing access to the mills on the Leicestershire bank of the Trent - sadly it is no more.

Swarkestone (Map 21)

Trent-side village featuring the CREWE & HARPUR (Tel: 01332 700641), a refurbished country inn and restaurant with accommodation. There are no shopping facilities other than a small garage on the A514, whose food shelves contained little more than spicy beef pasties on the occasion of our last visit.

There are glimpses from the canal of The Stand, an intriguing 17th century pavilion surmounted by a picturesque pair of ogee domes which is thought to have been used to accommmodate spectators as a grand-stand for viewing bear-baiting or jousting, though more probably simply bowls. There was once a great mansion here belonging to the Harpurs, who decamped to Calke. It is exactly the sort of charmingly enigmatic and idiosyncratic little structure which ought to have had covetous eyes laid upon it by the Landmark Trust (Tel: 01628 825925), a company of angels who make it their

business to reinvigorate unwanted treasures and make them available for holiday lets. And so it *has* - being able to accommodate just two people, tolerant enough to accept a bathroom approached by way of the roof terrace! For those partial to pop trivia, the Rolling Stones used The Stand as a backdrop for a photo-shoot in 1968.

Weston on Trent (Map 22)

Potentially confusing, this is the *second* Weston-on-Trent that the Trent & Mersey encounters on its travels - the other one being south of Stone.

Eating & Drinking

COOPERS ARMS - Weston Hall. Charming pub housed in 17th century mansion used by Cromwell as a temporary barracks. During the First World War an escaped German prisoner hid here briefly before eventually making his way back to his homeland. Tel: 01332 690002.
OLD PLOUGH - traditional village centre pub with a restaurant. Tel: 01332 700331.

NAVIGATION from the Trent to the Mersey must have seemed like a proclamation for travel from the earth to the moon, but this was how the fledgling canal company advertised its purpose back in 1780. The words adorn the largest warehouse at SHARDLOW, the company's 'inland port', once known waggishly as "Rural Rotterdam". And Shardlow, unlike its counterpart Preston Brook (Map 1), at the other end of the Trent & Mersey, has been fortunate enough to retain the greater part of its historic infrastructure. Pride of place goes to the handsome Clock Warehouse, now a popular pub, alongside Shardlow Lock. Like many of Shardlow's warehouses, it owes its survival to F. E. Stevens, a local animal feeds merchant, whose occupation of this, and several other canalside buildings, secured a use for them in the century which passed between the cessation of the local canal trade and a new era of refurbishment for leisure and commercial use.

Although it is Shardlow which appears on the distinctive Trent & Mersey mileposts, the actual junction with the Trent Navigation is at Derwent Mouth, approximately one and a half miles east of the village. It's a short journey, as easily accomplished on foot as afloat. Unfortunately, the imposing concrete horse-bridge, emblazoned with the initials of the Trent Navigation and dated 1932, which carried the towpath across the Trent opposite its confluence with the Derwent, was demolished in 2002 and had not been replaced by the time of our most recent visit - five years on! The Derwent looks alluring, but has not been navigable since the late eighteenth century.

Downstream the Trent, forming the boundary between Derbyshire and Nottinghamshire, sweeps haughtily towards Nottingham, an eye-opener for boaters passing through Derwent Mouth Lock and away from the cosy world of the canals. You pass beneath a pipeline which brings water supplies down from the Peak District to slake the thirst of Leicester folk, and you pass beneath the M1 motorway on which the traffic often seems to be moving more slowly than you.

As the Trent tumbles over a weir and passes beneath Harrington Bridge, a canalised cut brings you to Sawley Bridge Marina and its extensive facilities. East of here Sawley Locks are duplicated, automated and occasionally manned.

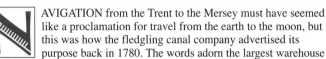

SHARDLOW
Heritage Clock Centre W'hse
Malt Shovel
New Inn 2
M
70
3
Lady in Grey
P
The Navigation

course of tramway

services

Dog & Duck

Shardlow

wharf

Tandoori

mp 3A
4
5
6
3
Aston Lock
8ft 1in

Shardlow Quarry

sand & gravel pits

Derbys.

River Trent

Shardlow
2
3
Shardlow Lock
4ft 5ins

Cavendish Bridge

maltings

Chinese

flood gate
2
mp

Shardlow Marina

River Trent

Chapel Farm Marina

sewage works

mp
1

1

Derwent Mouth Lock

River Derwent Derwent Mouth

water main

Notts.

M1 from The North

Sawley

Harrington Bridge

Weir !
floodlock

water

Sawley Marina (Canal Time)

golf course

Sawley Locks (dup)

21

B6540 to Castle Donington   M1 to London

Shardlow (Map22)

Attractive Georgian village much quieter now that the new A50 has siphoned off the heavy traffic that used to plague its main street. Shardlow Hall was built in 1684 by Leonard Forsbrook from profits made on the river trade. Small but interesting Heritage Centre on London Road. The maltings prominent by Cavendish Bridge house the Shardlow Brewing Company, 'Narrowboat' being one of their most popular brews.

Eating & Drinking

CLOCK WAREHOUSE - adjacent lock. Warehouse refurbishment popular with families. Marston's ales. Tel: 01332 792844.

LADY IN GREY - Bridge 2. Tel: 01332 792331. Thai-cooking.

THE OLD MARINA - Shardlow Marina. Tel: 01332 799797. Bar and restaurant.

THE NAVIGATION - London Road. Tel: 01332 792918.

THE NEW INN - The Wharf. Tel: 01332 793330.

THE MALT SHOVEL - The Wharf. Tel: 01332 799763.

DOG & DUCK - London Road. Tel: 01332 792224.

SHAKESPEARE INN - London Road. Tel: 01332 792728. Bar and restaurant.

OLD CROWN - Cavendish Bridge. Tel: 01332 792392. The only *Good Beer Guide* recommended pub (out of seven!) in Shardlow.

TANDOORI NIGHTS - London Road. Tel: 01332 853383.

GOLDEN DRAGON - Cavendish Bridge. Tel: 01332 799158. Chinese restaurant & takeaway.

Shopping

Post Office stores a mile west of the canal at Bridge 3. Newspapers from the garage.

Connections

BUSES run to Loughborough (via East Midlands Airport) and Derby - Tel: 0870 608 2 608.

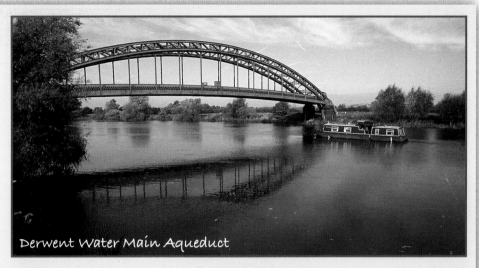

Derwent Water Main Aqueduct

Sawley (Map221)

Suburban sprawl to the north, but handsome church and core of original village near the river. Public footpath across the meadows and beneath the railway arches to Trent Lock.

Eating & Drinking

OLD CHANDLERY RESTAURANT - Sawley Marina. Tel: 0115 973 4278.

PLANK & LEGGIT - adjacent Sawley Marina. Tel: 0115 972 1515. All-day family orientated pub with 'Wacky Warehouse' play barn. Two meals for a tenner Mondays to Fridays.

HARRINGTON ARMS - Tamworth Road (adjacent church on B6540). Tel: 0115 973 2614. A worthwhile walk up from Sawley Marina, this *Good Beer Guide* regular serves excellent food.

THE WHITE HOUSE RESTAURANT - Tamworth Road. Tel: 0115 972 1261.

Trent Lock (Map 23)

Perennially popular 'resort' for day-trippers reached by non-boaters and towpath walkers along a no through road off the B6540.

Eating & Drinking

LOCK HOUSE TEA ROOMS - Tel: 0115 972 2288. Splendidly quaint and homely tea rooms overlooking the lock and famed for their knickerbocker glories: omelettes, salads, filled Yorkshire Puddings etc for the more savoury of tooth.

STEAMBOAT INN - Tel: 0115 972 6300. Refurbished pub by the Brtish Waterways/Scottish & Newcastle partnership. Outdoor decking overlooking the lock.

TRENT NAVIGATION - Tel: 0115 973 2984. All day pub with garden spilling down to the Trent.

ETWEEN the canalised 'cuts' of Cranfleet and Beeston the boater voyages upon the mighty River Trent, a watercourse not to be toyed with, especially when the current is running fast as is increasingly the case given the downpours associated with global warming. Red, yellow and green marker boards at the exits from the lock-cuts indicate when it is safe to proceed on to the river. Red - obviously - suggests you stay put, yellow urges caution, and green means that it is safe to go and that the river is in one of its gentler moods.

The Midland Main Line railway spans Cranfleet Cut under the shadow of Ratcliffe Power Station. Near here used to be the busy junction station known pithily as Trent. Another long-abandoned transport facility was a ferry at Thrumpton. Thrumpton Hall is the fine Jacobean mansion which featured in Miranda Seymour's memoir *In My Father's House*. On the southern horizon stands Gotham Hill and the village of Gotham, pronounced 'goat ham' and known once for the Merrie Tales of its Mad Men rather

than Batman and Robin. A pair of mineral tramways formerly existed to carry gypsum down to riverside wharves and a plaster works at Thrumpton.

From the boater's perspective, the river's high banks preclude much assimilation of the landscape, and one must focus instead on the waterside chalets and shanties, ranging from the sublime to the faintly ridiculous. Walkers and cyclists, on the other hand, are catered for by a well-maintained river path that connects with Attenborough's watery nature reserve, a valuable leisure facility based on former gravel workings where bitterns and otters are not unknown. Briefly, the Trent marks the boundary between Derbyshire to the North and Nottinghamshire to the south. Its tributary, the River Erewash, outfalls via the gravel flashes.

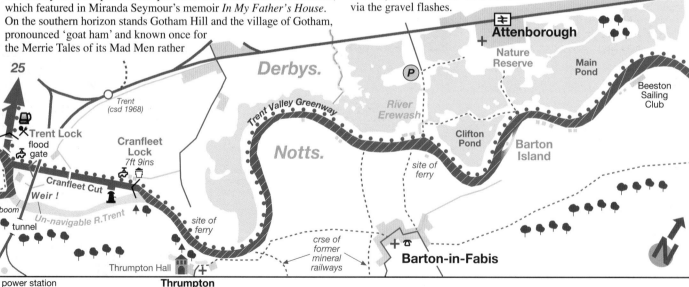

BEESTON CUT was dug towards the end of the 18th century to by-pass a tricky section of the Trent. Beeston Marina offers useful facilities including a chandlery that stocks a moderate range of groceries, a cafe and a licensed clubhouse. The cut acts as a defensive moat between Boots sprawling industrial estate and the acres of sports fields which separate it from the unnavigable Trent. You sense a good deal of industrial activity going on around you, but high banks of bindweed mask the bulk of this, so it comes as something of a relief to reach LENTON CHAIN and the Nottingham Canal. The Nottingham, from here northwards to its junction with the Erewash and Cromford canals at Langley Mill, was formally abandoned in 1937, though it had scarcely carried any traffic since the General Strike. Happily, from Lenton to the Trent, the Nottingham Canal is still very much in use and it forms a pleasant approach to the city centre. Nottingham Castle Marina and a large, waterside Sainsbury's supermarket

coincide with popular visitor moorings but we would encourage you to explore the full length of the canal through the centre of the city to Meadow Lane Lock as long as there hasn't been a significant fall of rain which might prevent access on to the river, a necessary manoeuvre in order to turn most craft. As you proceed, Nottingham opens up its arms in a welcoming embrace and, passing through Castle Lock, you come upon an impressive six-storey warehouse, still emblazoned with the legend **BRITISH WATERWAYS**,

continued on page 48

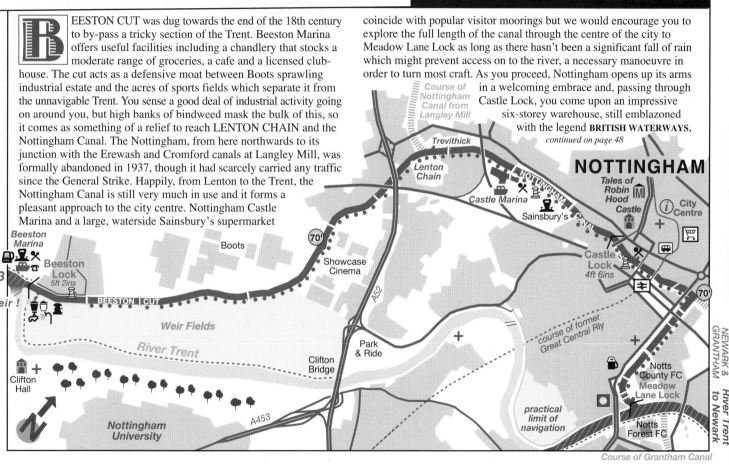

Course of Nottingham Canal from Langley Mill

Trevithick

Lenton Chain

Castle Marina

Sainsbury's

NOTTINGHAM CANAL

NOTTINGHAM

Tales of Robin Hood

Castle

City Centre

Castle Lock
4ft 6ins

Beeston Marina

Beeston Lock
5ft 2ins

BEESTON CUT

Weir !

Boots

70'

Showcase Cinema

A52

Weir Fields

River Trent

Park & Ride

Clifton Bridge

course of former Great Central Rly

70'

Clifton Hall

Nottingham University

A453

practical limit of navigation

Notts County FC

Meadow Lane Lock

Notts Forest FC

NEWARK & GRANTHAM River Trent to Newark

Course of Grantham Canal

23

continued from page 47

even though it has been converted to house bars and restaurants and fitness clubs rather than fulfilling its old role as a receptacle for goods delivered by water. One senses that the canal environment has been trivialised: on the opposite bank a roving bridge forms a sort of portcullis to the city's Magistatrates Court; an unfair sentence if ever there was one.

Passing under Carrington Street you snatch a glimpse of the terracotta frontage of Nottingham Midland railway station which dates from 1904 and has a distinct family likeness to Leicester. The rival Great Central Railway crossed the canal here too, its course aptly incorporated into Nottingham's relatively new and hugely successful tram network. Another lost railway, the Great Northern spanned the canal on a high level viaduct here, though most evidence of its existence has been swept away in an orgy of office and flat construction. Thus waterway and railway heritage intermingle as the canal makes a right-angle turn to the south and heads for the Trent. The GNR's handsome London Road (Low Level) station has become a health club: during the Second World War it was used by the Army as a sorting centre for mail, and it is claimed that one and a half million bags of love letters passed through its doors to sustain the fighting men's morale.

Running parallel with London Road the canal moves innocuously towards its destiny with the Trent. Though there are several overbridges, few offer access to and from the outside world. From one wharf hereabouts 'night soil' used to be despatched to Trentside farms for use as fertilizer. Notts County Football Club's Meadow Lane stadium peeps over an adjacent wall. Their history is not as illustrious as that of their neighbours Nottingham Forest, on the far side of the river, but at least they won the FA Cup - in 1894! The canal enters a quiet area of new housing where the effect is one of cloistered calm. The towpath peters out and only boaters are able to gain access to Meadow Lane Lock. Anything over fifty feet and you will have to pass through the lock to turn round. Your boat will probably enjoy the sense of liberation and want to loop the loop out of sheer *joie de vivre*. Or you might chug down to see where the old Grantham Canal once entered the Trent and Meadow Lane wharves where cargoes were unloaded within living memory.

Nottingham   (Map 24)

The city of Robin Hood and the late, much lamented Brian Clough; of lace and tobacco; of Sillitoe and Lawrence; of Boots and Raleigh; of Larwood and Hadleigh; is said to be populated by the prettiest girls in England. They used to work in the cigarette factories, nowadays they are more likely to work in the massive Inland Revenue offices which parallel the canal above Castle Lock!

Eating & Drinking

WORLD SERVICE - Castlegate. Tel: 0115 847 5584. Award-winning restaurant located in 17th century town house.
LE MISTRAL - Wheeler Gate. Tel: 0115 941 0401. Eclectic French cafe bar.
YE OLDE TRIP TO JERUSALEM - Castle Road. Reputedly England's oldest pub whose name derives from its use by Crusaders. Dates from 1189 but transcends 'ye olde' tackiness. Some rooms extend back into the sandstone rock topped by Nottingham Castle. Olde Trip house beer, lunches and no piped music! Tel: 0115 947 3171.

Shopping

Moor by the Magistrates Court and you are within minutes of the massive BROAD MARSH shopping centre. Further to the North stands the VICTORIA CENTRE (on the site of the old GCR station whose clock-tower it retains). In between are numerous pedestrianised shopping streets, malls and arcades of considerable charm and varying degrees of sophistication.

Things to Do

TOURIST INFORMATION - Smithy Row (adjacent Old Market Square). Tel: 08444 775678.
TALES OF ROBIN HOOD - Maid Marian Way. Tel: 0115 948 3284. Open daily, admission charge. Thrills and spills approach to the RH legend.
CITY OF CAVES - Broad Marsh. Tel: 0115 952 0555. Open daily, admission charge. Fascinating exploration with audio aids of Nottingham's underground labyrinth.
THE LACE HALL - High Pavement. Open daily, admission charge. Insights into the city's lace industry housed in 14th century building adjacent to the castle. Tel: 0115 941 3539.
GREEN'S WINDMILL - Sneinton. Tel: 0115 915 6878. One of Nottingham's landmarks, this working windmill churns out its own organic flour. open Wed to Sun and Bank Hols 10am-4pm. About quarter of an hour's walk from the canal - ask a policeman!

Connections

BUSES - Tel: 0115 950 6070.
TRAINS - Tel: 08457 484950.
TRAMS - Tel: 0115 942 7777.
TAXIS - Trent Cars. Tel: 0115 950 5050.

The Erewash Canal

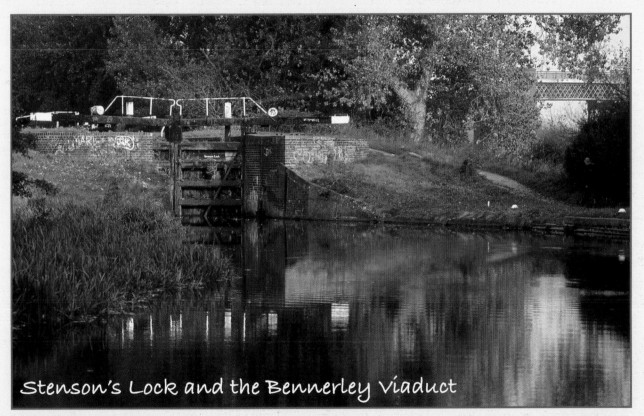

Stenson's Lock and the Bennerley Viaduct

THERE'S nothing quite like The Erewash anywhere else on the canal system. Twelve miles and fifteen widebeam, handcuffed locks ensconced in a predominantly urban landscape provide a recipe more likely to be savoured by the enthusiast than the holidaymaker. Such caveats notwithstanding, it's difficult to gainsay the surge of adrenalin which greets you as you come off the Trent into the entrance to the Erewash Canal at TRENT LOCK.

Firstly, though, in order to proceed any further, you'll have to procure a handcuff key, without which operation of the lock's paddle gear would be impossible. This suggests overtones of hooliganism, but we saw no evidence of this on our research trip to Langley Mill, the canal's terminus, and back. With hindsight we would have been better off with a couple of keys (they cost about 'a fiver' each) for ours led a charmed life being hurled from one side of each lock to the other by our two lock workers: luckily one had been a goalkeeper and the other a boundary fielder with a knack of holding high looping catches.

Don't expect to negotiate Trent Lock without an audience. The riverside hereabouts has long been a popular resort for East Midlanders, and two pubs, together with a tea room, continue to cater for this market. Ensuring that you've re-locked the paddle gear, you can now look forward to about two miles of lock-free cruising; time to come to terms with your initial impressions of the Erewash Canal. An almost surreal line of houseboats is first to catch your eye; one being impressively reminiscent of a Mississippi paddler. The picturesque Mills Dockyard follows, established as long ago as 1890. Two railway lines cross the canal then it passes the entrance to SHEET STORES BASIN, a group of imposing brick buildings once used by the Midland Railway for the manufacture and repair of wagon tarpaulins or 'sheets'.

School playing fields and a pretty park border the canal as it approaches LONG EATON. The lock is overlooked by a handsome cluster of lace mills housing staircases. characterised by semi-circular turrets of business here. The Textiles are still an important facet and the railway sidings mills give way to housing estates of their heyday when the of Toton; the latter a pale shadow marshalling yard was full of

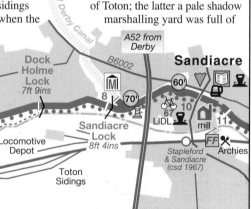

Nottinghamshire coal and the motive power depot was once of the largest in Europe. Toton was home to the massive Beyer-Garratt 2-6-6-2T locomotives introduced by the London Midland & Scottish Railway in 1927 specifically to haul heavy mineral trains along the Midland Main Line to London. Nowadays it belongs to the English Welsh & Scottish Railway whose brightly painted red and yellow diesels provide the haulage capacity for a good deal of Britain's rail freight.

Between Dock Holme Lock and Stanton, National Cycleway Route 67 adopts the canal's well maintained towpath. Pedestrians and anglers are apt to perceive cyclists as an unwarranted encumbrance, but towpaths provide potentially ideal off-road environments for bicycles and, to paraphrase the spirit of Rogers & Hammerstein's *Oklahoma*: 'canal folk should stick together, canal folk should all be pals'.

At SANDIACRE LOCK the keeper's cottage, dated 1779, has been taken over by the Erewash Canal Preservation & Development Association who open it to the public on Sunday afternoons. It was at this point that the Derby Canal formed a junction with the Erewash, the illusion of which remains by virtue of it being in water as far as the first overbridge. West of here part of it has been converted into a cycleway, though a Trust (*www.derbycanal.org.uk*) has been formed (see also Map 21) with a view to returning as much as is feasible to navigation in the future.

The busy A52 crosses the canal as it approaches SANDIACRE. Between bridges 10 and 11 the handsome Springfield mill has been fully restored, though as yet remained innocent of new usage when we last passed by.

Trent Lock (Map 25)

Perennially popular 'resort' for day-trippers reached by non-boaters and towpath walkers along a no through road off the B6540.

Eating & Drinking

LOCK HOUSE TEA ROOMS - Tel: 0115 972 2288. Splendidly quaint and homely tea rooms overlooking the lock and famed for their knickerbocker glories: omelettes, salads, filled Yorkshire Puddings etc for the less adventurous. STEAMBOAT INN - Tel: 0115 972 6300. Refurbished pub by the Brtish Waterways/Scottish & Newcastle partnership. TRENT NAVIGATION - Tel: 0115 973 2984. All day pub with garden spilling down to the Trent.

Long Eaton (Map 25)

Lace-making town which thrived with the coming of railways to the Erewash Valley. A fine shopping centre, though not necessarily somewhere to consider mooring overnight as the canal negotiates a canyon of factories.

Connections

BUSES - to/from Derby & Nottingham and along the Erewash Valley. Tel: 0870 608 2 608. TRAINS - frequent services to/from Derby and Nottingham plus through trains to London St Pancras. Tel: 08457 484950. TAXIS - Premier Taxis. Tel: 0115 939 3393.

Sandiacre (Map 25)

Suburb of Long Eaton with facilities easily reached from Bridge 10.

Eating & Drinking

ARCHIES - Bridge Street. Tel: 0115 949 9324. Contemporary British cusine with a seasonal emphasis in converted barn. Open for dinner

Long Eaton

Tue-Sat and Sunday lunches. *Several take-aways nearby.*

Shopping

LIDL 'supermarket' just east of Bridge 10. Butcher, post office and convenience store to west. Enterprising antique shop known as the GLORY HOLE also just east of Bridge 10 - Tel: 0115 939 4081.

A semblance of countryside intervenes between Sandiacre and Ilkeston: and thus Pasture Lock seems appropriately named; especially when one notices the remnants of 'ridge & furrow' patterns in canalside fields. Sandiacre's impressive parish church, St Giles, overlooks the valley from a prominent position on the adjacent ridge. Masked now by trees, nearby Cloud House belonged to an individual who made a small fortune operating barges on the Erewash Canal, in the house's early years he would have enjoyed a grandstand view over the canal artery, reassuringly replete with commerce.

The M1 motorway crosses the canal before it reaches Stanton (aka Junction) Lock. On our last research trip we were saddened to read in *The Times* that production of water pipes at the once giant Stanton Iron Works was soon to end - presumably the story had been leaked to the press. Tim Wilkinson described coming here with *Chiswick* and *Bawtry* to collect slag circa 1949 in his book *Hold on a Minute*, and how his wife Gay, a former model, beguiled the boat-loading manager into unprecedentedly filling the boats with slag on a Saturday afternoon - but, within a couple of years or so, regular trading on the Erewash Canal had ceased.

The Nutbrook Canal left the Erewash at Stanton (hence the lock's alternative name) and headed for four and a half miles through thirteen locks to Shipley. Despite the fact that it was abandoned due to subsidence over a century ago, odd sections of it remain in water, whilst its reservoir has become a surreal component of the American Adventure theme park.

The canal, negotiating locks at energy-sapping intervals, and running on the Derbyshire bank of the river from which it gets its name, skirts the fringes of Ilkeston, a hilltop town 'singularly devoid of visual attractions' in the rather blinkered and patronising opinion of Pevsner. Pearson, on the other hand, is traditionally more receptive to the places he encounters on his travels and trudged uphill on your behalf to discover a surprisingly busy and sizeable town of some thirty thousand souls, being especially entranced by the Erewash Museum (Tel: 0115 907 1141) with its fine displays of local transport history: canals, railways, trams and trolleybuses.

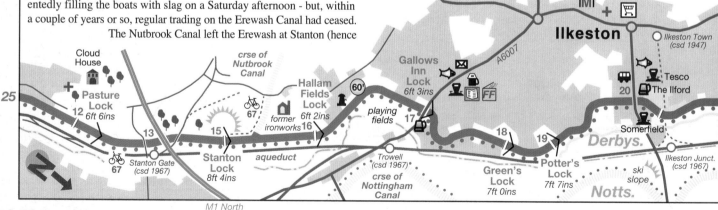

St. Giles, Sandiacre

LKESTON seems to accompany the canal for a very long time. It became a running joke with our crew. "Where are we now? - Still Ilkeston I think!" The town's football team, affectionately known as 'The Robins', play just down the road from Baker's Lock against a backdrop of domestic coal silos. Their history goes back as far as 1894. At Stenson's Lock we caught our fender in one of the top gates and jammed one of the gate paddles open. We drew solace from viewing the stupendous Bennerley Viaduct built by the Great Northern Railway in 1878 to carry their line from Nottingham to Derby across the Erewash Valley. Forged of wrought and cast iron, five hundred yards long and sixty feet high, it hasn't carried anything other than a ghost train in forty years, but still dominates the locality.

Ahead up the valley now you begin to catch glimpses of the towers of Heanor and Eastwood churches, the two hilltop towns which parenthesise Langley Mill on the valley floor. You are now entering D. H. Lawrence country, and in its still fragile sense of being half rural, half industrial, a very real ambience of the writer's landscape remains intact. The Nottingham to Chesterfield railway line crosses the canal, its track carrying a dwindling residue of its traditional traffic in Nottinghamshire and South Yorkshire coal. A railway milepost indicates that we are 128 miles from London St Pancras. The Great Northern Railway struck through the valley with a rival line now buried beneath the A610 dual-carriageway. Two railways, and *two* canals: as the Nottingham shadows the Erewash's

progress. A nicely wooded reach of canal culminates in a lily and reed-fringed winding hole.

By SHIPLEY LOCK there used to be a coal loading wharf. There was also a knacker's yard for worked-out canal horses. Just above the lock a small aqueduct carries the canal over the Erewash and at this point the canal becomes the boundary between Derbyshire and Nottinghamshire. From the recently rebuilt Bridge 26 a short walk to the east will bring you to a hump-back bridge over the course of the Nottingham Canal. The fruity aromas of a sewage works fill the air as the Erewash Canal essays its last lap into Langley Mill. There's a winding hole beyond Bridge 27, overlooked by a new business park, but most boaters will presumably want to climb through Langley Lock into the Great Northern Basin.

LANGLEY LOCK is, in fact, the first lock on the Cromford Canal which ran from Langley Mill to Cromford, a distance of fourteen miles. Infilled long ago north of Langley Mill, except for the last five miles between Ambergate and Cromford, the Cromford Canal must rank amongst the most disappointing canal casualties of the pre-leisure age, for beyond here it grew lovelier with each mile, delving into the foothills of the Peak District, traversing the much wooded valley of the Derwent, and encountering the celebrated

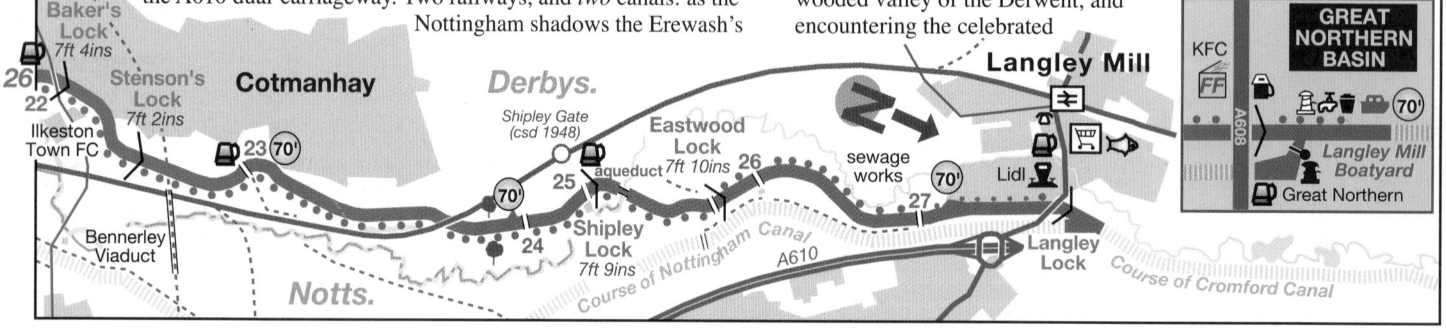

Map labels: Baker's Lock 7ft 4ins; Stenson's Lock 7ft 2ins; Cotmanhay; Ilkeston Town FC; Bennerley Viaduct; Notts.; Derbys.; 26; 22; 23 (70'); 24; 25; Shipley Lock 7ft 9ins; Shipley Gate (csd 1948); aqueduct; Eastwood Lock 7ft 10ins; 26; Course of Nottingham Canal; A610; sewage works; 27; Langley Lock; Langley Mill; Lidl; KFC; GREAT NORTHERN BASIN; A608; Langley Mill Boatyard; Great Northern; Course of Cromford Canal; 70'

Eastwood - Town Centre

Cromford & High Peak Junction Railway which had once been projected as a canal across the hills to Buxton and Whaley Bridge (see *Pearson's Canal Companion Cheshire Ring*).

GREAT NORTHERN BASIN was the unique meeting place of three canals, the third being the Nottingham Canal of which a small stub remains in use as moorings reached through an attractive swing-bridge. A restored pump house and a boatyard with a drydock complete the basin's infrastructure. Mooring here can be a pleasant experience. The natives are friendly, there are walks to be had along the courses of the Cromford and Nottingham canals, and of course one must not eschew a pilgrimage to Eastwood and David Herbert's birthplace museum.

Bennerley Viaduct

Langley Mill (Map 27)

Sethley Bridge in *Sons and Lovers*, this small valley floor community between the hilltop towns of Heanor and Eastwood used to be linked by the electric tramway so vividly brought to life in D. H. Lawrence's short story *Tickets, Please*. The tramway (and the trolleybuses which followed) are long gone and nowadays the A608 is busy with somewhat less desirable vehicles. Langley Mill itself lacks many airs or graces but is handily close to the basin for re-stocking the larder.

Canalside by the basin, the GREAT NORTHERN (Tel: 01773 713834) is a friendly local dispensing Greene King ales. Bar lunches Mon-Sat. Down in the centre you'll also find Indian and Chinese takeaways and a pizza parlour. Shops include a Netto supermarket, newsagent and post office. Frequent buses run to Heanor and Eastwood - Tel: 0870 608 2 608. Trains run to Nottingham and Chesterfield - Tel: 08457 484950.

Eastwood (Map 27)

Small town with much more character than Langley Mill, even in its state of post coal mining torpor. Notable chiefly for its close links with D.H. Lawrence, thus attracting literary pilgrims from all over the world. Good shopping facilities include a large Morrisons supermarket.
D. H. LAWRENCE BIRTHPLACE MUSEUM - Victoria Street. Tel: 01773 763312. Open daily, admission charge. Terraced house re-creating period feel of Lawrence's life and times. Souvenir shop with plenty of his novels on sale for reading as you wend your way back down the Erewash Valley. Quaint tearoom (called The White Peacock after Lawrence's first novel published in 1911) across the street and craft shops round the back. Local taxi services are provided by Eastwood Cars -Tel: 01773 770000.

The Staffs & Worcs Canal

Tixall Wide

Karen Tanguy

LARGELY unmolested, the canal slips quietly through the outskirts of Stafford. The county town stood an aloof mile to the west of the Staffs & Worcs Canal which, in true Brindley fashion, followed the easy contours of the Penk Valley. Plans to construct a branch were dropped in favour of a simple lock down into the Sow, the river being dredged and realigned to take boats as far as a terminal basin at Green Bridge in the centre of Stafford. The navigation was opened in 1816 and in use until the end of the First World War. A footpath follows the riverbank into the town, but it is difficult to imagine how seventy foot narrowboats ever got up there: all the old navigation needs now is a determined restoration society!

Baswich church once stood as isolated on its hillside as Acton Trussell's does still, but now it is surrounded by a housing development, though those with an interest in ecclesiastical architecture can easily reach it from Bridge 100. Note the spelling of the village's name with a 'k' on the bridgeplate. There was a substantial wharf by Radford Bridge, but its site is now somewhat less interestingly occupied by a car showroom following demolition of the original warehouses in the Philistine Seventies.

Stafford Boat Club - with their impressive club house and welcome

to visiting boaters - occupy a former brickworks arm near Hazelstrine Bridge. Most of the works's output was despatched by canal. Bridge 97 has disappeared completely, there being not even any tell-tale narrowing in the canal's channel where it once must have stood. Hereabouts the inherent other-worldliness of the waterway undergoes strange, paradoxical fluctuations in fortune. Nowhere could be more apparently remote than Deptmore Lock, where the reclusive inhabitant of the rose-clad cottages commutes to the outside world by dinghy. Elsewhere, however, the M6 threatens to intrude like an unwelcome caller on your afternoon off; whilst Acton Trussell, which you'd expect with such a name to be a picture book English village, disappoints with its banal modern architecture. Similarly Wildwood, which ought to be the home of friendly, furry little creatures straight out of some children's tale, has become a housing estate on a hill. But when vapours rise off the Penk, and its marshy meadows ooze sponge-like with excess water, a return to an older, more elemental existence seems somehow tangible, and man's scars upon the landscape recede into the mists of time.

Acton's houses attract a following of ducks. The solitary building on the towpath side used to be a boatman's pub. Present day boaters, however, slake their thirst in the old moated house by Bridge 92, opened a few years ago as a bar and restaurant set in charming grounds. It is said that Brindley actually used the old house's moat for a few yards when building the canal.

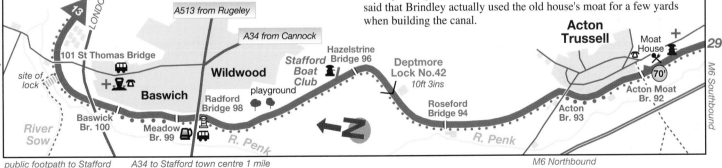

Stafford (Map 28)

One of England's lesser-known county towns, Stafford has always seemed too self-effacing for its own good; though there are signs that in recent years it has begun to wake up to its tourist potential. Unfortunately for canal folk, the centre lies over a mile from Radford Bridge. But there are frequent buses, and those with time at their disposal will find Stafford a rewarding place to visit. First stop should be the Ancient High House in Greengate Street - the main thoroughfare. Dating from 1595, it's thought to be the largest timber-framed town house remaining in England. Inside there's a heritage exhibition tracing Stafford's history since 913 when Ethelfleda, daughter of Alfred the Great, fortified the settlement against marauding Danish invaders. King Charles I stayed at High House in 1642, and in later years Izaak Walton visited relatives who owned it. An alleyway beguiles you off Greengate Street to discover the town's large parish church of St Mary, much restored by Gilbert Scott in the 1840s and containing the bust of Izaak Walton. Elsewhere, some impressive buildings reflect the town's administrative status, lending it on occasions an almost metropolitan air.

Eating & Drinking
RADFORD BANK - canalside Bridge 98. Pub and carvery. Tel: 01785 242825.
THE SOUP KITCHEN - Church Lane. Quaint, sprawling and recently extended eatery (enhanced by attentive waitresses) serving coffees, lunches and teas. Tel: 01785 254775.
STAFFORD ARMS - Railway Street. Real ale buff's pub serving Stoke-on-Trent brewed "Titanic" beers. Food and accommodation. Tel: 01785 253313.

Shopping
Good shopping centre featuring all the well known 'high street' names plus many attractive individual shops tucked away down twisting side streets. Large ASDA and TESCO supermarkets. Indoor market Tue, Thur, Fri & Sat. Farmers' Market on the second Saturday in the month. CO-OP 'Convenience Store' accessible from Bridge 100 at Baswich if you're just passing through.

Things to Do
TOURIST INFORMATION - Market Street. Tel: 01785 619619 *www.visitstafford.org*
ANCIENT HIGH HOUSE - Greengate Street. Tel: 01785 619131. Local history and gifts.
SHIRE HALL GALLERY - Market Square. Tel: 01785 278345. Exhibitions, crafts and coffee bar housed in an imposing late Georgian building overlooking the Market Square.
STAFFORD CASTLE - Tel: 01785 257698. Well preserved Norman castle on town's western outskirts.

Connections
BUSES - Tel: 0870 608 2 608.
TAXIS - AJ's Tel: 01785 252255.
TRAINS - Important railhead with wide variety of services. Tel: 08457 484950. Useful links with Penkridge and Rugeley for towpath walkers.

Acton Trussell (Map 28)

THE MOAT HOUSE - canalside Bridge 92, Acton Trussell. Four star hotel in former moated farmhouse: restaurant and bars, lovely gardens, customer moorings. Tel: 01785 712217.

Penkridge (Map 29)

Quite easily the best place to break your journey on the northern section of the Staffs & Worcs. Five minutes walk from the wharf will take you to the narrow main street, a pleasant spot to shop and saunter. At its foot stands an impressive church of sandstone, formerly a collegiate church, considered second only to a cathedral in ecclesiastical status.

Eating & Drinking
CROSS KEYS - canalside Bridge 84. A once isolated pub, described by Rolt in *Narrow Boat*, but now surrounded by a housing estate, though that doesn't diminish its popularity with boaters and motorists alike. Tel: 01785 712826.
THE BOAT - Bridge 86. Tel: 01785 714178. Canalside pub with an incongruous sign featuring a tanker barge on the Aire & Calder! FLAMES - Mill Street. Tel: 01785 712955. Contemporary Eastern cuisine.

Shopping
We sensed a downturn in the fortunes of Penkridge's independent retailers on our most recent visit, but the outdoor market on Wednesdays, Saturdays and Bank Holiday Mondays beside the river still apparently thrives.

Connections
BUSES - to Cannock, Wolverhampton and Stafford. Tel: 0870 608 2 608.
TRAINS - to Wolverhampton and Stafford. Tel: 08457 484950.

Coven (Map 31)

Coven's village centre is less than ten minutes walk from Bridge 71, but do take care crossing the A449!

Eating & Drinking
FOX & ANCHOR - canalside north of Bridge 71. Tel: 01902 798786. Flourishing Vintage Inns establishment offering a wide choice of food and drink. Fish & chip shop in the village centre and visitors welcome at the local golf course club house.

Shopping
Two food stores, pharmacy, post office, butcher, greengrocer and bakery.

AS the canal ascends to (or descends from) its summit level, the locks come thick and fast. The motorway retreats, only to be replaced by the housing estates which cling-wrap the otherwise agreeable little town of Penkridge. Yet, a mile on either side, the countryside is characterised by rolling farmland lifting to the bulwark of Cannock Chase.

The towpath between bridges 90 and 86 is hi-jacked by the "Staffordshire Way" which seems forever to be bumping into canals and appropriating towpaths in the course of its 92 mile journey from Mow Cop to Kinver Edge. Its route has come down off The Chase and crossed Teddesley Park. Teddesley Hall was the seat of Sir Edward Littleton, one of the chief promoters of the Staffordshire & Worcestershire Canal. Indeed, the family remained involved with the canal company until its nationalisation in 1947. The hall itself was demolished by the army in the mid Fifties (having been used as a prison camp for German officers during the Second World War) but the estate farm remains, hidden from the canal by some woodland known as Wellington Belt in commemoration of a visit to the hall by the Iron Duke. Bridge 89 once had ornate balustrades commensurate with its importance as the gateway to the hall, but sadly these have been infilled by ugly brickwork.

PENKRIDGE WHARF is quieter than of late, no longer being the location of a busy boat hire base. Boats still pause here to take on water, however, and there is usually room to moor up for a visit to the town. The Littletons had fingers in many pies, not least the local colliery, which at one time employed over a thousand men. A huge basin, now covered by the motorway, was constructed to enable boats to be loaded with coal from a raised pier by gravity. The chief traffic flow of Littleton coal by canal in later years was down to Stourport Power Station.

Rodbaston Lock had a keeper until the motorway was built. A special bridge was built over the new road to maintain access to his lockside cottage, but the noise of the ensuing traffic was so bad as to cause him to leave and find new accommodation, the cottage subsequently being demolished. West of the canal between Otherton and Rodbaston lies a college of agriculture.

Map labels:
- Rodbaston Br.80
- 30
- site of coly basin
- Rodbaston Lock No.35 — 8ft 6ins
- Otherton Lane Br.81
- Otherton Br.82
- Otherton Boat Haven
- Otherton Lock No.36 — 10ft 3ins
- c'rse of former colliery railway
- Lynehill Bridge 83
- N
- sch
- Filance Lock No.37 — 10ft 3ins
- 84   83A
- WOLVERHAMPTON
- Longford Lock No.39 — 10ft 0ins
- Broom Br.87
- 86 70' 85
- Penkridge Lock No.38 — 9ft 3ins
- A449
- Penkridge
- Teddesley Park Br.89
- Midland Chandlers Teddesley Boat Co. Park Gate Br.90
- Longford Bridge 88
- sch
- River Penk
- market
- STAFFORD   viaduct
- By-road to Brewood
- P Park Gate Lock No.40 — 7ft 6ins
- Shutt Hill Lock No.41 — 6ft 0ins
- Shutt Hill Br.91
- 28
- M6 Northbound

Tixall Lock

Park Gate Lock

Penkridge Lock

Karen Tanguy (K3)

C ALF HEATH is a strangely isolated tract of country, pancake flat and crossed by a grid of sullen little roads, with here and there a huddle of houses, gathered reassuringly together like something out of Van Gogh's early potato field paintings. The canal all but boxes the compass of this gravel pit-riddled landscape, so that The Chase with its communications tower and the chemical works with its phalanx of flaring chimneys, appear to move about you, teasing you into geographic insecurity, like a game of Blind Man's Buff.

The Staffs & Worcs Canal's summit - from Gailey to Compton - lies at more or less 340 feet above sea level. If you've climbed up from Penkridge and beyond it's a relief to be done with locks for the time being. Industry lines the canal at Four Ashes. The old tar works here was once served by Thomas Clayton boats.

The last load of Cannock coal came off the Hatherton Branch in 1949 and it was abandoned a couple of years later. However, the illusion of a junction remains, because the bottom lock (of what was once a flight of eight in three miles) is still used to provide access to moorings. The Lichfield and Hatherton Canals Restoration Trust is actively seeking restoration of the branch with the intention of linking it with the northern waters of the BCN at Norton Canes, and there is little doubt that its opening would prove a great fillip to the under-boated northern extremities of the BCN.

Watling Street crosses the canal at Gailey. The most significant feature here is the 'round house', originally a toll clerk's office but now a splendid canal shop run by mother and daughter team, Eileen and Karen Lester. There is something spell-binding about cylindrical buildings - Martello towers, windmills, lighthouses; even Birmingham's Bull Ring Rotunda - and Gailey roundhouse, in its lock-side setting, has a particular charm which begs to be captured on camera.

A short walk along the A5 will take you to Gailey Pottery, a small gallery and showroom housed in a former church. The pottery was established in 1976 by Paul Gooderham following his training at Wolverhampton Art College.

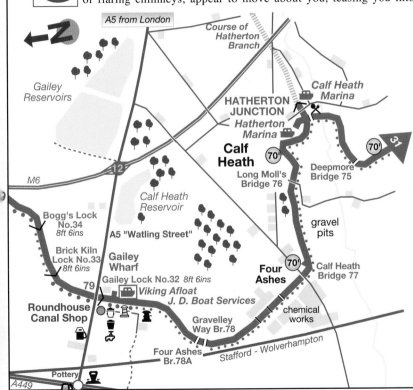

THE canal exchanges the loneliness of Calf and Coven heaths for the industrial and suburban outskirts of Wolverhampton; the M54 to Telford forming an obvious, though not intentional, boundary. At Cross Green a former boatman's pub called "The Anchor" has become the "Fox & Anchor", a popular restaurant bar, and many boaters choose to moor here overnight. As it passes beneath the M54 the canal crosses the county boundary between Staffordshire and the West Midlands, one of the new counties which had its origins in the local government changes of 1974. Many people still mourn the old counties. It must have been galling, for instance, to have lived in Lincolnshire all one's life and wake up one morning in South Humberside. West Midlands was possibly the dullest of all the new names, and sounds as though it must have been the compromise of a committee. Black Country would have been a far more appropriate and resonant title. You can imagine its inhabitants

espousing a perverse pride in such a name, no-one could possibly show a flicker of interest in anyone who admitted to coming from the West Midlands! The most significant feature of this length is "Pendeford Rockin", the old boatmen's name for a shallow, but tellingly narrow cutting hewn by Brindley's navvies through a solid belt of sandstone which breaks through the clay strata at this point. The cutting, half a mile or so long, restricts the channel to such a degree that you begin to wonder if you have lost concentration and taken a wrong turn. There are, however, one or two passing places - as on a single lane road - where oncoming boats can be successfully negotiated without losing one's temper. As the canal moves towards Autherley Junction it skirts the perimeter of a large school, screened from the waterway by a long line of poplar trees which have the look of teachers sternly trying to keep order at Morning Assembly.

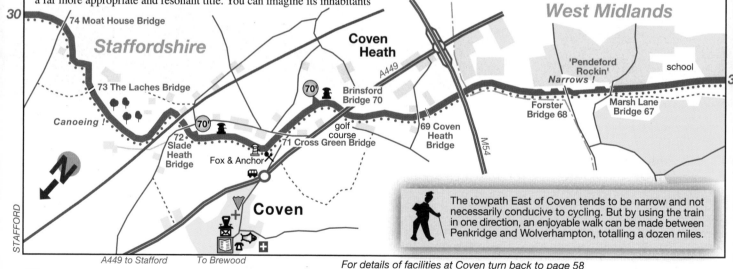

The towpath East of Coven tends to be narrow and not necessarily conducive to cycling. But by using the train in one direction, an enjoyable walk can be made between Penkridge and Wolverhampton, totalling a dozen miles.

For details of facilities at Coven turn back to page 58

The Shropshire Union Canal

Shroppie Country

D ESPITE the proximity of Wolverhampton, Autherley, like many canal junctions, is self-contained. It is not pretty in a conventional sense, being bordered by housing estates, sewage plants and public open spaces. In typically pithy fashion, the old boatmen called it 'Cut End', for the obvious reason that the Shropshire Union Canal began and, more pertinently, ended here. Once there was all the paraphernalia of a meeting of waterways: toll office, stables, workshops, employees cottages, and a dominant, sweeping roving bridge carrying the Staffs & Worcs towpath over the entrance to the Shropshire Union. A stop lock - just six inches deep - protected the two companies' precious water supplies. Much of this infrastructure survives, enjoying a new lease of life in the leisure age as a hire base and boatyard.

A massive sewage plant provides the canal with much of its water; suitably treated of course, or perhaps this explains the Shropshire Union's apparent impatience to get on with its journey to the north-west. Whatever the motivation, Autherley is soon forgotten as the canal crosses the boundary between the West Midlands and Staffordshire and leaves the housing estates of suburban

Wolverhampton behind. The land east of the canal was once occupied by an aerodrome, whilst the works by Bridge 4 was formerly an aircraft factory, turning out, amongst other designs, the 'Defiant' fighter plane.

An 'invisible' aqueduct carries the canal over the little River Penk before the waterway goes through a series of contortions which see it narrowing, then widening, then narrowing again before resuming its usual width beyond Bridge 6. John Liley, in his largely, yet unjustly neglected *Journeys of the Swan* (George Allen & Unwin 1971) considered that 'evening is the finest, certainly the most mysterious, time to enter this canal'; and as the *Swan* progressed through Brewood to Wheaton Aston and beyond, he half expected to encounter a highwayman at each bridge. Temporarily, the M54 impinges on such romantic illusions, but otherwise the landscape is as thus evoked, setting the scene for the forty mile journey to Nantwich through some unexpectedly remote countryside.

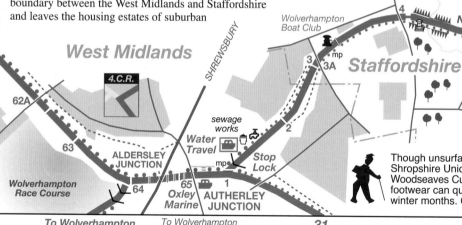

Though unsurfaced for a considerable proportion of its length, the Shropshire Union towpath (with the notable exception of Woodseaves Cutting - Map 38) can be comfortably walked, though footwear can quickly become wet and muddy, especially in the winter months. Cyclists may find the going bumpy in places.

THE Shropshire Union slices through the Staffordshire countryside in cuttings and upon embankments typical of the bold, 19th century designs of Thomas Telford, who engineered this route between Autherley and Nantwich, originally known as the Birmingham & Liverpool Junction Canal. Travelling northwards you rapidly become attuned to the unique atmosphere of this canal. Far from becoming monotonous, its purposeful, loping stride across the landscape is strangely exhilarating, perhaps due to the recurring contrast of shadowy cuttings and panorama providing embankments, known as 'rockings' and 'valleys' respectively to past generations of boatmen.

There are two notable structures either side of Brewood. To the south the distinctly ornate, balustraded Avenue Bridge (No 10) carries the carriageway to Chillington Hall. The advent of the canals heralded many similar attempts at ornamentation and disguise, where powerful landowners would only condescend to permit a waterway to cross their parklands if suitable steps were taken to adorn the otherwise purely functional architecture of the new trade route. In contrast, north of Brewood, the canal crosses the old Roman Road of Watling Street on a sturdy, yet elegant aqueduct of iron, brick and stone construction. Nearby Belvide Reservoir is one of the main sources of water supply for the Shropshire Union Canal, whilst Broom Hall, east of Bridge 16, was the home of William Carlos who hid King Charles II in the oak tree at nearby Boscobel after the Battle of Worcester in 1651.

Brewood

Probably because it is so close to the county boundary, Brewood feels more like Shropshire; there being a 'West Country' richness about it that doesn't pertain, for example, to nearby Penkridge. And there really is a timelessness about 'Brood' which seduces you into spending longer here than you might have planned. Winding lanes of gracious houses lead to the old market place where the distinctive, and often venerable vehicles of the Green Bus Company pause before rumbling off to Wolverhampton. Enhancing one corner of the square is 'Speedwell Castle', a Gothic fantasy erected in the 18th century on the winnings of a racehorse named Speedwell.

Eating & Drinking

BRIDGE INN - Bridge 14. Much extended former boatmans' pub. Tel: 01902 851999. Banks's, Marston's & guest ales. Home cooked food. *Good Beer Guide* entry.

THE MESS - Market Place. Tel: 01902 851694. Daytime cafe and evening restaurant. www.the-mess.co.uk

Shopping

Old fashioned shops where you can eavesdrop on local gossip: baker, butcher, chemist, newsagent with post office counter, SPAR (with cash machine) and branch of Lloyds TSB Bank. COOPERS foodstore is excellent, as is the VILLAGE BAKERY for filled baps.

Connections

BUSES - Frequent Green Bus Co services (Mon-Sat) to/from Wolverhampton; some run through to/from Wheaton Aston and are thus useful for one-way towpath walks. Tel: 0870 608 2 608.

WHEATON ASTON Lock is strangely solitary - the only one in 25 miles of canal; a telling statistic of Telford's engineering. For about a mile the canal penetrates the deciduous heart of Lapley Wood, and there's another typical Shroppie cutting by Little Onn, but elsewhere the embankments offer wide views eastwards towards Cannock Chase.

How astonishingly remote and unpeopled the landscape seems. The West Midlands conurbation is less than a dozen miles to the south, yet moor for the night between Wheaton Aston and Little Onn, and you'll have only the occasional eerie hoot of a hunting owl, or the distant silent wash of headlights on a country lane, for company.

Abandoned wartime aerodromes inevitably have their ghosts, and in decay accumulate a patina of lore and legend, hard perhaps to equate with the often mundane use to which they were put after closure. Wheaton Aston was opened in 1941 and became one of the RAF's largest training units, operating a squadron of 'Oxfords'. There were at least two canal dramas. Once an American 'Thunderbolt' crash-landed in the waterway. Another well remembered wartime incident occurred at the lock when a narrowboat, carrying an unsheeted cargo of shining aluminium on a moonlit night, was attacked by a German aircraft which unleashed a bomb that exploded less than a hundred yards from the chamber. Swords into ploughshares: after the war the aerodrome became a pig farm!

(Map)

Coach & Horses — Ivory Cottage

Wheaton Aston

Spar
Hartley Arms
70'

Lapley Wood Cutting

stop gate

18
19 mp 20

aqueducts

20a
20b
20c mp

stop gate

former WWII aerodrome

Little Onn
Hall

Wheaton Aston Lock 7ft 0ins

17
mp

21
22
23
mp 24

Rye Hill Cutting

"Staffs Way" to/from Penkridge

By-road to Penkridge

33

Wheaton Aston

Once purely a farming community, Wheaton Aston has been overwhelmed by modern housing. So it's certainly no picture postcard village, but at least it appears to be thriving, defying the trend towards rural decline.

Eating & Drinking
HARTLEY ARMS - canalside Bridge 19. Popular pub offering a good range of food. Tel:

01785 840232.
IVORY COTTAGE - High Street. Tel: 01785 840702. Indian restaurant/ take-away.
COACH & HORSES - village centre. Old fashioned Banks's local which also offers Chinese take-aways! Tel: 01785 841048.

Shopping
Post office, newsagents, plus excellent SPAR opposite the church. It's open daily

7am-10pm and, along with all the other to be expected requisites, does a nice line in spit-roasted chickens, fresh-filled baguettes, and ready-to-eat pies and pasties.Turner's quaint canalside garage stocks Calor gas, diesel and boating accessories. FR eggs from Bridge Farm.

Connections
BUSES - Services to/from Brewood, Wolverhampton. Tel: 0870 608 2 608.

THE buildings of two wharves remain intact at High Onn. One - now converted into a most desirable home - belonged to Cadbury's, the other to a local landowner, suggesting that there was once a degree of agricultural traffic on the canal. Deep shadowy sandstone cuttings, spanned by lichened grey stone bridges of simple balance and unaffected beauty, lead to the eighty-one unlined yards of Cowley Tunnel; the only one on the Shropshire Union. Once a dizzy jungle of trees darkened the approaches so much that you were never quite sure where the tunnel began and the cutting ended, but their roots caused instabilities in what was already a brittle rock strata and they were felled in 1985.

On a clear day the embankments north of Gnosall reveal that famous Shropshire landmark, The Wrekin, 15 miles to the south-west; a slumbering hunchback of a summit, 1335ft high. A. E. Housman celebrated it in *A Shropshire Lad*, and Salopians raise their glasses in a toast to: "All friends around the Wrekin".

Now in use as a public footpath, the dismantled railway line which crossed the canal at Gnosall once usefully connected Stafford with Shrewsbury until a certain doctor made his presence felt. Historically it was unusual in that it was actually built by the Shropshire Union Canal Company, apparently hedging their bets on the transport mode of the future. When, in 1846, they leased themselves to the London & North Western Railway, few shareholders would have backed the canal to outlast the railway as it has done.

former milk depot **Lord Talbot's Wharf**
well 70' 26
25 mp 27
28
Joan Eaton's Cross
29 30 mp
Chamberlain's Covert
Home Farm
31 32
A518 from Newport
Navigation
mp 34 35 35A 36
Cowley Tunnel No.33
Gnosall Heath
The Boat
former flour mill
Millennium Way (Course of Stafford - Shrewsbury railway)
Royal Oak
37
36
stop gate

Gnosall

This appendage of Gnosall (No-zull) grew up with the coming of the canal. Two pubs slaked the thirst of passing boatmen, a steam powered flour mill took advantage of the new transport mode, and a non-conformist chapel kept a sense of proportion amidst all the excitement. Nowadays the pubs pander to pleasure boaters and passing motorists and the flour mill and chapel have become private residences.

Eating & Drinking

THE BOAT - Bridge 34. Marston's/Banks's pub with attractive curved wall abutting the bridge. Food available and pleasant garden by the water's edge. Tel: 01785 822208.

THE NAVIGATION - Bridge 35. Nice garden with good children's playground. Tel: 01785 822327.

ROYAL OAK - Newport Road. Tel: 01785 822362. *Good Beer Guide* recommended alternative. Fish & chips on A518 open daily (except Sundays), both sessions. Tel: 01785 822806.

Shopping

General store (with cash point) and butcher by Bridge 34.

Connections

BUSES - Arriva services to/from Stafford and Newport. Tel: 0870 608 2 608.

Bridge 26

rd Talbot's Wharf

Water Point,
near Knighton

Autumn Colours

69

A MASK of tall trees disguises the immensity of Shelmore embankment. It was six years in the making and, in its way, was as glorious an engineering feat as any of Telford's more visibly imposing aqueducts. A vast army of navvies and horses was employed on it. Spoil from the big cuttings at nearby Gnosall and Grub Street was brought by wagon for its construction. To Telford's dismay the earthworks slipped time after time and, as the rest of the canal was finished, Shelmore stubbornly refused to hold. In poor health, Telford struggled to oversee its completion, conscious that the bank need not have been tackled at all, had Lord Anson of Norbury Park sanctioned the preferred course through Shelmore Wood. Sadly, Norbury is no longer a junction, though the name lives on. How nice it would be to lock down the 'Seventeen Steps' of the Newport Branch and head across the marshy emptiness of Shropshire's Weald Moors to Shrewsbury. A feasibility study recently put a cost of £86m on fully restoring the canal.

North of Norbury lies Grub Street cutting. For over a mile the canal is wrapped in a thick coat of vegetation, again, like Shelmore, hiding the sheer size of the eighty foot deep cutting, whose most unusual feature is the double-arched bridge which carries the A519 across the canal. The tiny telegraph pole is a survivor from the line which once marched beside the Shroppie for much of its length. Ironically, canals are again being used as lines of communication with the burying of optical fibres beneath selected lengths of towpath. It is to be hoped that this hi-tech activity meets with the approval of the black, monkey-like creature reputed to have haunted Bridge 39 ever since a boatman was killed here in the 19th century. Grub Street Cutting has recently had its towpath upgraded to good effect: thankfully, it is no longer necessary to equip yourself with a pair of fisherman's waders to negotiate it.

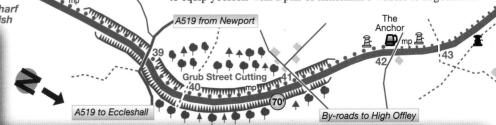

Course of Newport Branch Canal

Shelmore Embankment — Norbury Junction — Junction Inn — **Norbury** — BW — 70' — Old Wharf Tea Rooms — 38 — *Norbury Wharf Anglo Welsh* — mp — *A519 from Newport* — The Anchor — mp — 39 — *A519 to Eccleshall* — Grub Street Cutting — 40 — 41 — 42 — 43 — 70' — *By-roads to High Offley*

Norbury Junction
An atmospheric canal community, and although the suffix is misleading nowadays, Norbury remains a busy canal centre where British Waterways have a maintenance yard. Some of the houses are still occupied by canal workers.
Eating & Drinking
JUNCTION INN - canalside Bridge 38. Busy pub popular with boaters and motorists alike. Garden with children's play area. Bar and restaurant meals. Tel: 01785 284288. Gift shop in garden.

ANCHOR INN - canalside Bridge 42. Famously unspoilt boatman's pub serving Devizes-brewed Wadworth 6X from the jug. Gift shop to rear selling souvenirs and T-shirts. Tel: 01785 284569.
OLD WHARF TEA ROOMS - canalside Bridge 38.

All-day, all year licensed cafe; sizeable portions of homely cooking. Tel: 01785 284292.
Shopping
Boatyard shop: provisions, off-licence, gifts, chandlery and a good choice of canal books.

CROSSING the border between Staffordshire and Shropshire, the canal continues to traverse an uncluttered countryside almost entirely given over to agriculture. It can come as a surprise to find so remote a landscape in the 'crowded' middle of England. One is tempted to categorise the area as 'lost' but for the obvious truth that it has never been 'found' in the first place.

Blithely we pleasure boaters sail across embankments and through cuttings with no more thought for their construction than if we were driving down the M6. But imagine the impact of Telford's brash new canal on the surrounding early nineteenth century landscape. Put yourself in the position of Sir Richard Whitworth's tenant farmer at Batchacre Park. Up until 1830 dawn rose across the open pasturelands throwing light through his east-facing windows. A year later his view of the rising sun was cut off forever by an embankment twice the height of the farmhouse. No wonder the landowners of this rural corner of Staffordshire had their misgivings, and the canal company paid dearly in compensation for the land they acquired.

West of the canal, there are good views of The Wrekin, with the Clee and Breidden hills prominent on the far horizon. It comes as something of a surprise to encounter a confectionery factory in the midst of otherwise empty countryside. It was opened by Cadbury, the chocolate manufacturers, in 1911 as a centre for processing milk collected from the dairy farming hinterland of the Shropshire Union Canal. Canal transport was used exclusively to bring countless churns gathered from numerous wharves along the canal; from simple wooden stages at the foot of fields, to the sophistication of Cadbury's own plant at High Onn. Cadbury owned a distinctive fleet of narrowboats, being one of the first operators to experiment with motorised craft. Cocoa and sugar crumb were also brought by boat to Knighton and blended with milk to make raw chocolate, itself returned to Bournville, again by boat, to be transformed into the finished delicacy. The last boatman to trade to Knighton was Charlie Atkins senior; nicknamed 'Chocolate Charlie' for obvious reasons. He carried the final cargo from Knighton to Bournville in 1961. Since then all transport to and from the still busy works has been by road. Attempts to have the handsome Art Deco type canalside buildings demolished have, thus far at least, been staved off by a preservation order.

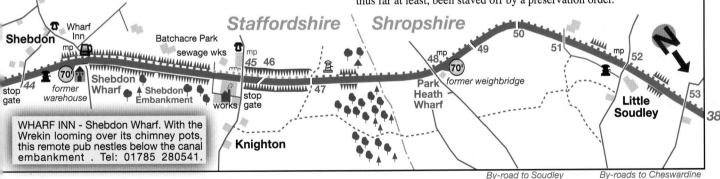

WHARF INN - Shebdon Wharf. With the Wrekin looming over its chimney pots, this remote pub nestles below the canal embankment . Tel: 01785 280541.

By-road to Soudley   By-roads to Cheswardine

THE Shroppie flirts with the county boundary, the towpath forming the demarcation so that, technically, the canal lies briefly in Staffordshire. The landscape, though, is impervious to the machinations of local government, remaining aloof and typically remote: a tall, dark, silent canal, this Shropshire Union.

WOODSEAVES is another prodigious cutting. The canal narrows and, in places, is cut through solid rock. These cuttings proved just as troublesome to Telford and his contractors as did the embankments. There were frequent avalanches during construction and, even today, brittle lumps of sandstone are inclined to dislodge themselves and tumble into the canal; one reason why a 2mph speed limit is imposed. Well-shod walkers will be grateful for the cool shade on hot days - cyclists might find the going all but impossible: though improvements are, apparently, in the pipeline. A feature of Woodseaves is its pair of high bridges, spanning the canal like portals to the mysterious chasms of another world. In a poem called *Don't Forget the Woodseaves Giants*, Rod Dungate (better known as a playwright) likens them to cathedral vaults, and suggests that in Woodseaves Cutting, 'time seems stripped of its power'.

At TYRLEY (pronounced 'Turley') a flight of five locks - the last to be faced southbound for seventeen miles - carries the canal down into, or up out of, Market Drayton. The lower chambers are located in a shadowy sandstone cutting across which branches intertwine to form a tunnel of trees. Damp and rarely touched by sunlight, all manner of mosses and ferns flourish in this conducive environment. After dusk bats leave their tree bole roosts to hunt for insects, acrobatically twisting and turning over the luminous pounds between the locks.

TYRLEY WHARF was a point of discharge and collection for the local estate at Peatswood; Cadburys also used to collect milk from here and take it by boat to their works at Knighton. The buildings date from 1837 and were erected in a graceful Tudor style by the local landowner. Nowadays, its commercial significance a thing of the dim and distant past, it would be difficult to imagine a more picturesque scene though it is sad that the craft shop and home-baking outlet, admirable enterprises of the 1980s, have both been and gone.

Summary of Facilities
Remote from any village, THE WHARF TAVERN by Bridge 55 is a popular port of call throughout the boating season and features a spacious canalside garden. Tel: 01630 661226. Ten minutes west of Tyrley Wharf (past Tyrley's reticent little redbrick church) you'll come upon THE FOUR ALLS - Tel: 01630 652995 which offers bar and restaurant meals and also accommodation.

By-road to Cheswardine

ayton Wharf

yrley Wharf

Hotel Boats
on the
Middlewich Branch

73

ARKET DRAYTON was the largest, in fact the only, town encountered by the old Birmingham & Liverpool Junction Canal on its route from Autherley to Nantwich. Naturally, a sizeable wharf was provided for dealing with local cargoes; though the canal's monopoly on local trade lasted only thirty years before the railway reached the town. It is sometimes difficult, in these days of the ubiquitous juggernaut, to appreciate the importance of the canal wharf and the railway goods yard to the past prosperity of small towns like Drayton. They must have been the hub of local life, few businesses would have been able to carry out their trade without regular recourse to the wharfinger and the stationmaster. From the opening of the canal until the First World War no commodity, apart from local agricultural produce, could have arrived at Market Drayton, or been dispatched, without the involvement of these important gentlemen. On the canal a large basin and a sizeable warehouse and adjoining cornmill remind us of this lost significance.

Pleasant 48 hour moorings, bordered by school playing fields, stretch

south from Bridge 62 to the imposing aqueduct over the lane to Peatswood. Steps lead down to the road below, which crosses the little River Tern nearby and forms the most romantic, but not the most convenient, approach to the town centre.

By Bridge 65, H. Orwell & Son have added boatyard facilities to their traditional business as coal merchants. Note the substantial stone abutments where the North Staffordshire Railway once crossed the canal. Another long lost railway accompanies the canal past Adderley.

BETTON CUTTING is not among 'The Shroppie's' most dramatic, but it is reputed to be haunted by a shrieking spectre, and working boatmen would avoid lingering here in the old days. Indeed, it could be said that this whole canal has something of a fey quality about it, a blurring of past and present which is liable to send shivers down susceptible spines.

The ADDERLEY flight is neat and tidy, although not the place it was when every chamber was bordered by flower beds and the grass manicured like a bowling green. A privet hedge beside the third lock down indicates the site of a demolished lock-keeper's cottage, one of many to have disappeared from the canal system over the years.

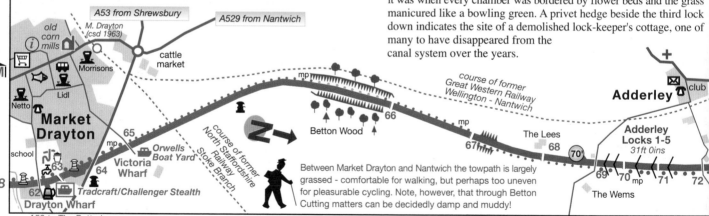

Market Drayton

The conspicuous Second World War pillbox guarding Bridge 62 is not, despite first impressions, still in situ as a deterrent to visitors. Self-styled as 'The Home of Gingerbread', Drayton is best visited on a Wednesday when the ancient market is in full swing and country folk gather to seek out a bargain and a gossip. This is the town's real heritage, along with its half-timbered houses which mostly date from the aftermath of a fire which swept through the place in 1651. Drayton's most famous son was Robert Clive, best remembered here for scaling the sturdy tower of St Mary's and for blackmailing local shopkeepers - ideal escapades in preparation for a career in diplomacy and military leadership. He established British rule in the Sub Continent and became known as 'Clive of India'. Betjeman and Piper's Shell Guide of 1951 recalls that the district was once terrorised by a murderous gang known as 'The Bravoes of Market Drayton'. On Saturday nights, as the pubs empty, it's easy to believe they are still at large. To the west of the town lie the large premises of Muller - 'the UK's most loved dairy product brand' - whilst on the northern fringe is Drayton's Livestock Market, a flourishing centre for agricultural buying and selling.

Eating & Drinking
THE TALBOT - adjacent Bridge 62. Tel: 01630 654989. A handsome, red brick Georgian inn just east of the canal. Accommodation available.
STAFFORD COURT HOTEL - Stafford Street. Tel: 01630 652646. Bar & restaurant food in small, but well-appointed town centre hotel.
THE BUTTERCROSS - town centre tea room: coffees & teas, oatcakes & omelettes. Tel: 01630 656768.

Shopping
It isn't easy for small market towns to compete these days, let alone small independent shops, but Market Drayton does its best and still bustles on a Wednesday, market day. WILLIAMS OF WEM is a fine delicatessen beside the handsome Buttercross. Branches of all the main banks, a post office, launderette and Lidl, Morrisons, and Netto supermarkets will cater adequately for most boaters' requirements.

Things to Do
TOURIST INFORMATION - Cheshire Street. Tel: 01630 653114 www.marketdrayton.gov.uk

MUSEUM - Shropshire Street. Tel: 01630 657455. Open Wednesdays, Saturdays and Sunday (afternoons) from April to October. Admission free. Local history nostalgically displayed in an old shop.

Connections
BUSES - X64 services approximately bi-hourly, daily to/from Stoke and Shrewsbury, with one bus operating to/from Audlem on market day - useful for one-way towpath walks. Tel: 0870 608 2 608.
TAXIS - First Call Taxis. Tel: 01630 653200.

The Buttercross

Karen Tanguy

FIFTEEN locks running through a cutting of larch and Scots pine take the canal across the Shropshire/Cheshire border. The locks are well-maintained and a pleasure to operate. Vegetables and fruit are often available from an honesty box by Lock 9. The barrel-roofed building by Lock 10 was used by stonemasons, blacksmiths and carpenters engaged in maintaining the flight. Towards the foot of the flight - known to old boatmen as the Audlem "Thick" - you pass Audlem Wharf, one of the prettiest ports of call on the Shropshire Union, with a former warehouse restored as a popular pub and the adjacent lofty mill converted into a superb craft shop.

North of the bottom lock, below which is a well preserved stable block used as a base by the Daystar Theatre Group, the canal, wide with concrete banking but deceptively shallow, bounds across the infant River Weaver on a high embankment. One of the crazier notions of the Ministry of War Transport during the Second World War was to make the Weaver navigable by 100 ton barges to this point, beyond which a lift would carry them up to the level of the Shropshire Union, upgraded sufficiently for them to travel as far south as Wolverhampton. Pleasure boaters can be thankful that this scheme never got off the drawing board and can moor at the foot of the Audlem flight in splendid isolation.

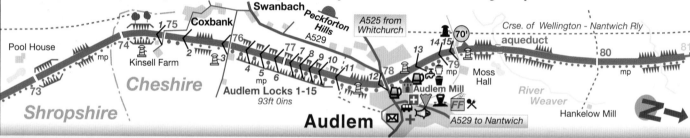

Audlem

"The sleepers sleep at Audlem" sang Flanders and Swann in *Slow Train*, their elegy for the Beeching cuts, and whilst they were referring to the village's station and its imminent closure, Audlem remains a sleepy place. Now that the trains have gone and the average motorist is hell bent on getting somewhere else as fast as he can, only the canal traveller is journeying at a pace to do justice to this lovely village, highpoints of which are the ancient buttermarket and parish church.

Eating & Drinking

THE BRIDGE - canalside Bridge 78.

Marstons, food. Tel: 01270 811267.
THE SHROPPIE FLY - canalside Lock 13. Nicely furnished warehouse conversion serving bar and restaurant meals. Tel: 01270 81772.
THE LORD COMBERMERE - The Square. Refurbished village centre pub. Tel: 01270 812277.
THE PLAICE - Cheshire Street. Fish & chips.
OLD PRIESTS HOUSE - The Square. All day breakfasts, coffees, teas and light lunches.
KEBABLAND - Tel: 01270 812226. Take-away.

Connections

BUSES - services to/from Nantwich and Whitchurch on weekdays. Tel: 0870 608 2 608.

Shopping

Friendly shops cater for most needs and make shopping here a pleasure rather than a stressful chore. Many shops indulge in a lunchtime siesta though, and Wednesday is half-day. Ice cream, produced on the premises, is available from the old fashioned confectioners by the market cross. Cash machine at the Co-op. Audlem's outstanding establishment, however, is the AUDLEM MILL CANAL SHOP converted from the three-storey Kingbur Mill by John Stothert in 1976. After thirty years, John has retired, and the mill is now under new ownership: a hard act to follow, we wish them well!

AT Hack Green there are two isolated locks and the remnants of a stable, recalling the practice of frequent changing of horses on the 'fly' boats which travelled day and night with urgent, perishable cargoes. This is the Cheshire Plain and dairy farming has long been a vital part of the area's economy - though for how much longer one might wonder, given the precarious state of agriculture at the beginning of the 21st century. We tend to think of farming as an unchanging facet of the landscape, but the Friesian cattle synonymous with milk production would have seemed like interlopers to 19th century boatmen more used to indigenous British breeds like Ayrshires and Alderneys.

Unchanging landscape! Thank goodness this is comparatively true, for when we first explored this canal in the early Eighties we were blissfully unaware of Hack Green's nuclear bunker, a Second World War radar station secretly designated to play a role as a Regional Government Headquarters in the event of a nuclear war. Deemed redundant at the end of the Cold War, it has somewhat bizarrely become a tourist attraction:

fascinating stuff, but more than a little unnerving too.

Adroitly changing the subject, let us recall how trade survived on this canal until the 1960s; which must be some sort of testimony to the viability of canal carrying. Perhaps in the final analysis attitudes rather than economics prevailed. One of the most celebrated traffics on the Shroppie in latter years was Thomas Clayton's oil run from Stanlow on the banks of the Mersey to Langley Green, near Oldbury in the Black Country. The contract commenced in 1924 and the Clayton boats, with their characteristic decked holds, and river names, were a mainstay of trade on the canal for thirty years. Even post-war, a thousand boat-loads per annum were being despatched from Stanlow, some remaining horse-drawn until the early Fifties. But, in common with other canals, the Shropshire Union lost its final freights to the motor lorry; then, for many, with the disappearance of its working boats, something died on the Shroppie, some intangible component of canal heritage that no amount of preservation, nor hectic holiday trade, can ever compensate for.

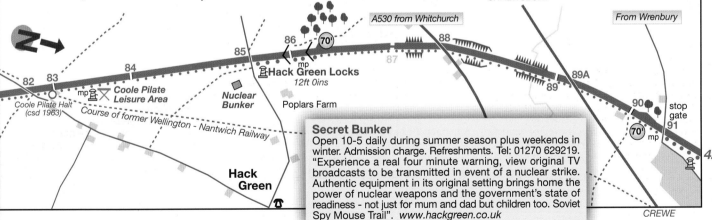

Secret Bunker
Open 10-5 daily during summer season plus weekends in winter. Admission charge. Refreshments. Tel: 01270 629219. "Experience a real four minute warning, view original TV broadcasts to be transmitted in event of a nuclear strike. Authentic equipment in its original setting brings home the power of nuclear weapons and the government's state of readiness - not just for mum and dad but children too. Soviet Spy Mouse Trail". www.hackgreen.co.uk

THE character of the Shropshire Union Canal changes perceptibly at Nantwich: northwards lie the broad, winding waters of its earlier constituent, the Chester Canal, opened in 1779; southwards the direct and narrow Birmingham & Liverpool Junction Canal, upon which work began here in 1827, though five years elapsed before the embankment settled sufficiently for the canal to be opened. Northbound, it's easy to feel lost without the reassuringly regular appearance of those elegant mileposts which have accompanied you from Autherley.

Long before the advent of the canals, Nantwich was reduced to ashes by the Great Fire of 1583 which lasted for almost three weeks. Four bears, thoughtfully released for their own safety, are said to have 'considerably hampered' attempts to douse the flames! Concerned for the area's salt industry, Queen Elizabeth donated a thousand pounds towards the town's rebuilding fund. Sixty years later Nantwich sided with the Parliamentarians during the Civil War, the only Cheshire town to do so. In 1644 its citizens were besieged by the Royalists for six weeks. An annual re-enactment celebrates their relief on the 25th January.

The broad embankment elevates the canal above the housing, back gardens and allotments which constitute the periphery of Nantwich. Ironically, these earthworks, together with a cast iron aqueduct over the Chester road, could have been avoided if the owners of Dorfold Hall had not objected to the passage of the canal across their land. A Sculpture Trail has been laid out beside the embankment's refurbished towpath, the main exhibit being in the form of a boat horse built out of reclaimed lockgates. Visitor moorings are provided along the length of the embankment, and they make for a pleasant overnight stay with easy access to the town centre, an enjoyable ten minutes to the east.

The basin and former terminus of the Chester Canal, indicating the more expedient route to the south which Telford would have liked to have used, nowadays provides further valuable mooring space, long term and short term, and there is a certain pleasure to be had from manoeuvring in and out of its narrow confines: all a far cry from 1939 when Tom and Angela Rolt couldn't get *Cressy* into the basin because a bar of silt, built up by the passage of motor boats, prevented their entry. Adjoining the basin are the premises of the Nantwich & Border Counties Yachting Club, an organisation whose founder members were early advocates of the use of the canal system for leisure.

Between Nantwich and Hurleston Junction (Map 43) the former Chester Canal passes uneventfully through a landscape typical of the Cheshire Plain.

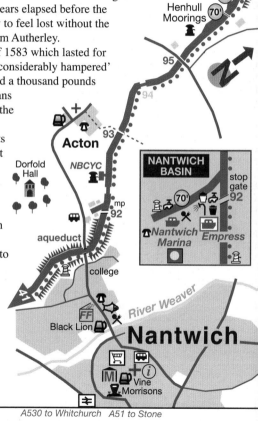

Henhull Moorings

Acton

Dorfold Hall

NBCYC

mp 92

aqueduct

NANTWICH BASIN

stop gate 92

Nantwich Marina

Empress

college

River Weaver

Black Lion

Nantwich

Vine
Morrisons

A530 to Whitchurch   A51 to Stone

Nantwich

The octagonal tower of St Mary's church, glimpsed across freshly-built rooftops from the high canal embankment, tempts you to moor and get to know this picturesque and historic Cheshire town. Walking in from the basin, the aqueduct forms an appropriate portcullis, and the appeal of the town increases as the centre is reached. Few English towns are cleaner or better endowed with floral displays. In medieval times Nantwich was the chief salt producing town in the county. Elizabeth, wife of John Milton, of *Paradise Lost* fame, was buried in the grounds of the town's first Baptist Chapel in 1727. For a brief Victorian heyday Nantwich flourished as a spa town. On closer inspection, there are bullet holes in the fabric of the church, where traitors and spies were executed by firing squad during the Civil War.

Eating & Drinking

BLACK LION - Welsh Row. Tel: 01270 628711. *Good Beer Guide* recommended 17th century half-timbered pub on way into town. Weetwood ales from nearby Tarporley.

McCORMICK'S - Pepper Street. Tel: 01270 628451. Lively coffee house and sandwich bar.

VINE INN - Hospital Street. Tel: 01270 624172. Hydes ales and a good menu.

CURSHAWS - Welsh Row. Tel: 01270 623020. Stylish modern eaterie on way into town.

BON AMIS - Hospital Street. Tel: 01270 628347. Amiable French bistro at the far end of the town.

Shopping

More affluent than Market Drayton, Nantwich's antique shops and boutiques emphasise its position at the centre of a well-heeled hinterland. But it is perhaps the food sellers that are most satisfying: butchers like CLEWLOWS (whose pork pies are 'to die for'), bakers like

Summer Showers, Henhull

Karen Tanguy

CHATWINS (whose headquarters are in the town) and fishmongers like SEA BREEZES (whose fish is fortunately *not* that local) all of whom have branches in Pepper Street. NANTWICH BOOKSHOP overlooks the Town Square and is an excellent independent with a coffee lounge upstairs where you can dip into any newly acquired reading matter. On Hospital Street make a bee line for WELCH, a butchers, grocers, delicatessen and coffee merchant. Across the street, there's SOUNDS MUSICAL a good dealer in classical, jazz and world music CDs, whilst on Pillory Street there's a fine wine merchant. A market is held on Tuesdays (mornings), Thursdays and Saturdays, whilst Wednesday is half day closing. On the way back from town it's difficult to resist the siren call of BARLEYCORN'S beer shop! Laundry facilities are available at the canal basin.

Things to Do

TOURIST INFORMATION - Civic Hall. Tel: 01270 610983.
www.crewe-nantwich.gov.uk
NANTWICH MUSEUM - Well presented displays of local history. Free admission.
Tel: 01270 627104.

Connections

BUSES - Tel: 0870 608 2 608.
TRAINS - services to/from Crewe and Shrewsbury. Tel: 08457 484950.
TAXIS - Direct. Tel: 01270 585000.

URLESTON and Barbridge are the 'Clapham Junctions' of the inland waterways. Throughout the cruising season the section between them is often frenetic with boats converging and diverging to and from all points of the canal compass. Providentially the old Chester Canal was built to barge dimensions and there is usually plenty of room to manoeuvre. Bridge 98 used to carry the weight of milking herds bound for the neighbouring parlour. Now this has been converted into housing and the pastures given over to maize; a sobering reflection on the profit & loss of agriculture.

HURLESTON JUNCTION, with its quartet of locks, is the starting point of the Llangollen Canal's serene journey into Wales; a route fully covered in our *Welsh Waters Canal Companion*. It's overlooked by a high-banked reservoir which receives its water supplies from the Llangollen Canal, a factor instrumental in the survival of the waterway back in 1944 when there were proposals to close it.

BARBRIDGE JUNCTION marks the beginning and end of the Middlewich Branch of the Shropshire Union Canal, and it is, along with Middlewich, Great Haywood and Autherley, a pivotal point for all Four Counties Ring travellers. On this map we include the length of canal up to Bunbury simply for the benefit of boaters journeying to or from the boatyard there. Notwithstanding the A51's thundering traffic, Barbridge is a popular overnight mooring spot, with two pubs vying for custom. And there's the interest of the junction itself, where once a transhipment shed spanned the main line. You can detect its site where the canal narrows just south of the junction. Rebuilding it would be a worthwhile heritage project.

Summary of Facilities
Both the OLDE BARBRIDGE INN (Tel: 01270 528443), Bridge 100, and the JOLLY TAR (Tel: 01270 528283), opposite the junction: the former offers 'Two Meals for a Tenner', and Jazz on Thursday evenings; the latter Country & Western on Saturday nights. BUSES run from stops at Wardle linking Chester and Crewe via Nantwich. Tel: 0870 608 2 608.

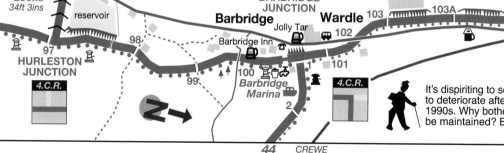

It's dispiriting to see how the towpath has been allowed to deteriorate after extensive refurbishment in the early 1990s. Why bother with improvements unless they can be maintained? Budgets slashed one imagines!

REMOTE, and seemingly always windswept, the Middlewich Branch of the Shropshire Union cuts across the grain of the landscape on a series of high embankments. It can be a busy length of canal for, as well as Four Counties Ring traffic, it funnels boats to and from the hugely popular Llangollen Canal, consequently its four deep and heavy-gated locks can become bottlenecks at the beginning and end of summer weeks.

Historically, the branch, opened in 1833, belonged to the Chester Canal Company and was engineered by Thomas Telford. Trade was heavy in cargo-carrying days, as after opening of the Birmingham & Liverpool Junction Canal this became the optimum route between the Black Country and the industrial North-west. Trade also developed between Ellesmere Port on the banks of the Mersey and The Potteries: Cornish china clay in one direction, finished crockery in the other. In 1888 a curious experiment was undertaken, to see if it was feasible to replace horse-power by laying a narrow gauge railway along the towpath below Cholmondeston Lock, and employing a small steam locomotive called 'Dickie' to haul strings of narrowboats. The concept didn't develop here, laying track was considered cost-prohibitive and there were problems in steering the boats,

though it did catch on abroad, especially on the French waterways. Cholmondeston still retains a railway presence, however, in the shape of the Crewe to Chester line, part of the historic route of the Irish Mails to Holyhead.

A high wooded embankment carries the canal across the River Weaver. Four Counties Ring travellers meet the river again near Audlem. It rises on the south-facing slopes of the Peckforton Hills and passes beneath the Llangollen Canal at Wrenbury prior to becoming navigable at Winsford, less than five miles downstream of the Weaver Aqueduct. There is nothing spectacular about the canal's crossing of the river, but it takes place in the most agreeable of locations. And, as you pass on your elevated way, it's hard to escape a fleeting sense of regret that the riverbank, being on private land, cannot so easily be explored.

Summary of Facilities
Venetian Marina incorporates a tea room, gift shop and extensive chandlery. Tel: 01270 528251.

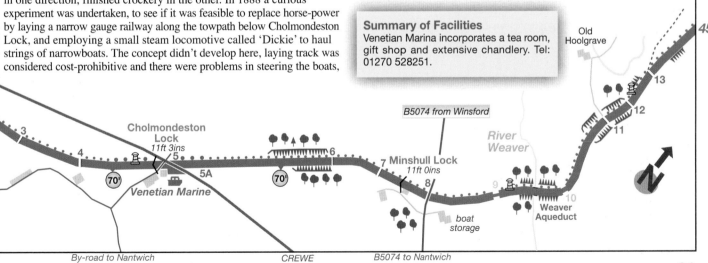

45 SUC MIDDLEWICH BRANCH

Church Minshull 4mls/0lks/1hr

TO subconsciously relegate the Middlewich Branch to the back of your mind as an unspectacular, but necessary link in the waterways of the North-West would be unjust, for this is a rumbustious canal, extrovertly ushering you loftily above the snaking valley of the Weaver, presenting you with expansive views towards a horizon bounded by Delamere Forest and the Peckforton Hills. Church Minshull - all russet coloured brick and black & white half timbering - looks, from the canal's elevated position, like a toy village embracing the river's luxuriant banks. Tom and Angela Rolt enjoyed an extended stay here in the fateful Autumn of 1939 while Tom worked for Rolls Royce at Crewe. It was tedious work he didn't enjoy, but the couple revelled in the close-knit community which flourished at Minshull: the blacksmith who shod the local cart horses; and the miller whose water wheels supplied the village with its electricity, continuing to do so right up until 1960.

Several sizeable farms border the canal, their fields filled with dairy herds or cut red by the plough in a ruddy shade of corduroy. Near Bridge 22, woods partially obscure the Top Flash, a subsidence induced lake beside the Weaver. The main London-Glasgow railway crosses the canal, its sleek electric trains swishing by at thirty times the speed of your boat. To the south-east lies a forgotten, older transport route, a Roman road which linked the early salt mines at Nantwich and Middlewich. Some interesting old canal horse stables have been converted into living quarters by Bridge 18.

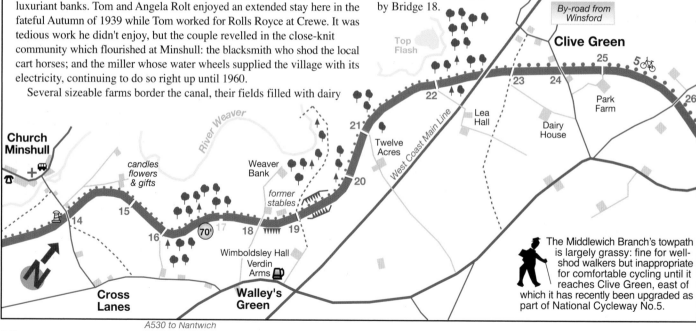

The Middlewich Branch's towpath is largely grassy: fine for well-shod walkers but inappropriate for comfortable cycling until it reaches Clive Green, east of which it has recently been upgraded as part of National Cycleway No.5.

82

The Caldon Canal

Light and Shade on the Leek Arm

RUNNING through the upper valley of the Trent, a narrow, lacklustre stream difficult to equate with the river that this guide encounters at Derwent Mouth, the Caldon Canal struggles to extricate itself from the urbanisation of The Potteries. When fields do finally appear they seem shaggy and unkempt, as though this were a no-man's land between true countryside and town. Near Milton a short arm once led to Ford Green ironworks and Smallthorne Colliery, both vanished. Engine Lock recalls the existence of a pumping engine in the vicinity of Cockshead Colliery. At Norton Green the Knypersley Feeder (long ago navigable to a remote colliery basin) joins the canal. Knypersley is one of three reservoirs, along with Stanley and Rudyard, which feed into the Caldon, and thence the Trent & Mersey. The fledgling Trent is piped beneath the canal by Bridge 22. The Stockton Brook flight carries the canal forty feet up to its summit level of 486ft. Stone walls and small holdings begin to create a Pennine sense of obduracy.

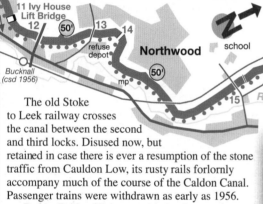

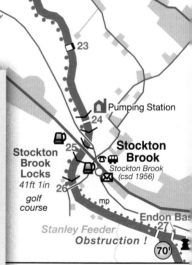

The old Stoke to Leek railway crosses the canal between the second and third locks. Disused now, but retained in case there is ever a resumption of the stone traffic from Cauldon Low, its rusty rails forlornly accompany much of the course of the Caldon Canal. Passenger trains were withdrawn as early as 1956.

Before Bridge 27 an unusual circular metal platform obstructs the centre of the channel, marking the site of a light-railway swingbridge. Endon Basin, once used as a transhipment point from rail to canal for Cauldon Low limestone, is now occupied by Stoke Boat Club.

Ivy House Lift Bridge is operated with the use of a BW key. Make sure that the barriers are fully down before attempting to operate the bridge using the push button controls. Lift-bridges 21 and 23 require winding up and down with a windlass.

Summary of Facilities
Milton is a lively little frontier post, a last chance for meaningful shopping until you reach Leek; always assuming you're going that way. Good moorings, friendly pubs and an exceptional village bookshop (Abacus - Tel: 01782 543005) add to its appeal. There are two butchers, a pharmacy, off-licence, KwikSave and a Co-op with a cash machine. Chinese take-aways on 01782 534966. Frequent buses to/from Hanley. From Bridge 21 a lane leads to a nice little pub at Norton Green called the FOAMING QUART. Two contrasting pubs might tempt you to tarry at Stockton Brook, though it is difficult to moor in the flight. THE SPORTSMAN is a Marston's local; THE HOLLYBUSH is a refurbished all-day pub. The Post Office sells newspapers.

onic Kilns
Hanley

bandoned Railway
Northwood

THINGVELLIR

Ivy House
Lift Bridge

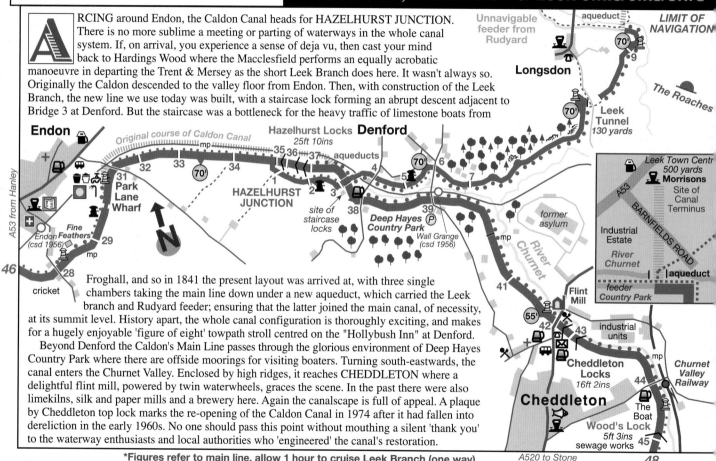

RCING around Endon, the Caldon Canal heads for HAZELHURST JUNCTION. There is no more sublime a meeting or parting of waterways in the whole canal system. If, on arrival, you experience a sense of deja vu, then cast your mind back to Hardings Wood where the Macclesfield performs an equally acrobatic manoeuvre in departing the Trent & Mersey as the short Leek Branch does here. It wasn't always so. Originally the Caldon descended to the valley floor from Endon. Then, with construction of the Leek Branch, the new line we use today was built, with a staircase lock forming an abrupt descent adjacent to Bridge 3 at Denford. But the staircase was a bottleneck for the heavy traffic of limestone boats from

Froghall, and so in 1841 the present layout was arrived at, with three single chambers taking the main line down under a new aqueduct, which carried the Leek branch and Rudyard feeder; ensuring that the latter joined the main canal, of necessity, at its summit level. History apart, the whole canal configuration is thoroughly exciting, and makes for a hugely enjoyable 'figure of eight' towpath stroll centred on the "Hollybush Inn" at Denford.

Beyond Denford the Caldon's Main Line passes through the glorious environment of Deep Hayes Country Park where there are offside moorings for visiting boaters. Turning south-eastwards, the canal enters the Churnet Valley. Enclosed by high ridges, it reaches CHEDDLETON where a delightful flint mill, powered by twin waterwheels, graces the scene. In the past there were also limekilns, silk and paper mills and a brewery here. Again the canalscape is full of appeal. A plaque by Cheddleton top lock marks the re-opening of the Caldon Canal in 1974 after it had fallen into dereliction in the early 1960s. No one should pass this point without mouthing a silent 'thank you' to the waterway enthusiasts and local authorities who 'engineered' the canal's restoration.

*Figures refer to main line, allow 1 hour to cruise Leek Branch (one way).
for details of facilities at Endon & Cheddleton turn to page 91

The Leek Arm

From Hazelhurst, the branch to Leek curves away from the main line which locks attractively down to pass beneath it. Two overbridges precede a sharp turn at the site of the old staircase locks before the branch then crosses the main line on an imposing brick aqueduct dated 1841. A lesser aqueduct over the railway follows before the branch settles down on the opposite hillside for the delightful journey to Leek. Winding, dipping in and out of overbridges, and passing some envy-provoking waterside properties, the canal traverses a gorgeous belt of woodland, full of bluebells in spring, where jays screech mockingly amongst the tree tops and brackeny banks spill down into the valley of the River Churnet. Presently the view ahead opens out towards the high flanks of The Morridge rising to 1,300ft in the east, whilst glowering over your right-hand shoulder stands the spooky tower of Leekbrook Asylum. If the inmates weren't deranged before they were incarcerated here, they would probably be sent mad by the sheer despondency of the hospital's grim institutional architecture, ironically now transformed into exclusive housing.

All of a sudden the canal encounters a remote pool enclosed by low hills - one of the most idyllic mooring spots on the whole system. The canal builders had no alternative but to dig a tunnel in order to reach Leek. The confined 130 yard bore is fronted by an ornate portal of red sandstone. Walkers take the horsepath across the top and are rewarded by stunning views over the town to the The Roaches beyond.

Less than a mile of canal remains in water. The final turning point for all but the smallest cabin cruiser is just beyond Bridge 9. Around the corner the canal peters out as its feeder comes in from Rudyard, three miles to the north. A public footpath (part of the "Staffordshire Way") follows the feeder to the reservoir which gave us Kipling's Christian name. An aqueduct, dated 1801, once carried the canal across the Churnet to reach a terminal wharf nearer the town centre. The aqueduct remains but is bereft of water, whilst the bed of the canal lies beneath an industrial estate. A sad loss to this now tourist-conscious town, although the creation of a country park here has done much to enhance the setting of the current terminus.

Leek *(Map 47)*

Full of sudden architectural treats, Leek is tucked away from the outside world in deep folds of the Staffordshire Moorlands, conforming to everyone's mental image of a typical northern mill town. In fact it is an entertaining and evocative place to explore, and canal travellers are entitled to mourn the disappearance of the old terminal arm and the resultant bleak trudge through an industrial estate which forms their initial, and definitely misleading, impression of this magically self-sufficient little town.

Eating & Drinking

GREYSTONES - Stockwell Street. Tel: 01538 398522. Absolutely brilliant tearooms in beautiful 17th century house. Open Weds, Fris & Sats.
LEEK OATCAKE SHOP - Haywood Street. Tel: 01538 387556.
CAFE DAVIDE - Getliffes Yard. Tel: 01538 372255. Brasserie, wine bar & coffee shop.
RAYMONDO'S - Russell Street. Tel: 01538 381190. Open Wed-Sun from 7pm for dinner.
DEN ENGEL - Stanley Street. Tel: 01538 373751. Belgian beer cafe.
BOLAKA SPICE RESTAURANT - Stockwell Street. Tel: 01538 373734.

Shopping

All facilities can be found in the town centre a mile north-east of the canal, though there is a large MORRISONS store nearer at hand. The outdoor market is held on Wednesdays, but the charming little indoor Butter Market additionally functions on Tuesdays, Fridays and Saturdays. The delight of shopping in Leek lies in the proliferation of small shops offering individuality and personal service such as COUNTRY CUISINE (Tel: 01538 384455) in Sheepmarket Street, a friendly delicatessen and bakery. There is a good new/secondhand bookshop on Stanley Street. Leek is also enjoying a burgeoning reputation as a centre for antiques. A number of the textile mills operate factory shops selling their products direct to the public.

Things to Do

TOURIST INFORMATION CENTRE - Market Place. Tel: 01538 483741.
BRINDLEY MILL/JAMES BRINDLEY MUSEUM - Mill Street. Small admission charge. Open Easter- September Sat, Sun & BH Mons 2-5pm. Open same hours Mons, Tues & Weds in late July/August. Restored water powered corn mill built by James Brindley in 1752. www.brindleymill.net

Connections

BUSES - frequent service to/from Hanley and connections with Cheddleton and Froghall. Tel: 0870 608 2 608.
TAXIS - Malkins. Tel: 01538 386797.

Forty Winks
Oakmeadow
Ford Lock

Ornamental Ironwork
Hazelhurst Junction

Himalayan Balsam
on the Leek Arm

Lonely Waters
Leek Tunnel Pool

48 CALDON CANAL

BEYOND Cheddleton the enchantment deepens as the Caldon engenders an almost Amazonian sense of solitude. Briefly, in a distant echo of the arrangement at Alrewas (Map 16) the canal merges with the River Churnet at OAKMEADOW FORD LOCK, though there is little change of character, other than when heavy rainfall causes the river current to increase its normally sluggish pace - check the gauge to ensure that it is sensible to proceed!

You begin to wonder why on earth they ever bothered to build a canal in such an extraordinarily remote outpost of Staffordshire. But this is a countryside with plenty of skeletons in its closet. Haematite iron ore and limestone were extensively mined in the area, and there were also several coal shafts and flint-grinding mills. At its zenith in the 1860s, an average of thirty boats a day were carrying ore out of the Churnet Valley.

The Caldon Canal was promoted for two main reasons: for the export of limestone from Cauldon Low; and to provide the summit of the Trent & Mersey with extra water. It opened in 1779, but was literally the death of James Brindley, who caught pneumonia on a surveying trip with fatal consequences for that genius of the early canal era.

Reaching CONSALL FORGE, the river disengages itself from the canal, disappearing over a weir to race ahead down the valley. The canal, however, makes light of this snub, passing under the railway, once a picturesque byway of the North Staffordshire Railway, now a preserved

line. The channel grows noticeably more slender, so that the passing of oncoming boats becomes a matter of discretion and a little 'give and take'. Squeezing past the cantilevered waiting room of Consall's beautifully restored station, the canal descends through FLINT MILL LOCK, at the tail of which a 'loading gauge' reveals whether or not your boat will pass through the confines of Froghall tunnel. Cherry Eye bridge recalls, it is said, the inflamed, bloodshot eyes of the neighbourhood's ironstone workers.

A concreted section of canal follows as an embanked length prone to breaching is negotiated. Woodland tumbles down to the water's edge on one side, whilst on the other, an equally steep descent leads to the river. Suddenly a factory wall looms out of the trees, heralding the formerly vast copper wire works of Thomas Bolton & Sons. The factory dates from 1890 and once operated a small fleet of narrowboats, though most of its transport needs were supplied by the railway. It was turned over to munitions during the war and apparently the Luftwaffe tried to bomb it but couldn't find it; which is not surprising when you take into account its position in this amphitheatre of heavily wooded hills. Much of the site is being redeveloped as housing; a metaphor for much of post-industrial England.

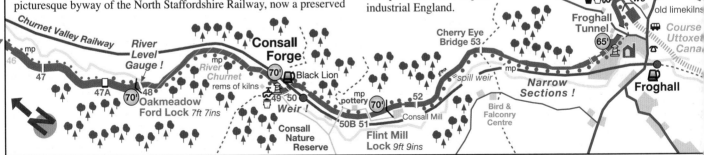

ourney's end is frustratingly foreshortened for ome boaters by the restricted bore of Froghall unnel. A winding hole is provided by the copper orks. British Waterways have recently carried ut remedial work to enable more boats to queeze through the tunnel. If, your boat con-ormed to the loading gauge (roughly 5 feet quare above the water line) you can proceed to e picturesque terminal which lies beyond. The est of us must follow the path around the side.

The peace and quiet of FROGHALL BASIN oday is hard to reconcile with the busy basin here limestone, brought down by plate tramway om the quarries, was cut to size and loaded on narrowboats. Here were sidings, great banks f limestone, smoking kilns, and, significantly, e top lock of the Uttoxeter extension, opened 1811. It proved financially unviable and when e North Staffordshire Railway acquired the rent & Mersey system they quickly closed it own and built a railway over much of its irteen mile course. Now, of course, the railway as gone the way of the canal, though it has been onverted into a delightful bridleway between akamoor and Denstone.

Meanwhile, back at Froghall, the top lock has een refurbished to provide access to a new ooring basin. Over seventy-five years have assed since the wharf was abandoned ommercially, and in the intervening period ature has reclaimed her own. A picnic site is ow located in the shadow of the lime kilns and trip boat operates from the old wharf building. everal signposted walks can be enjoyed in the icinity, or you can just laze by the canal, aking in the setting's remarkable feeling of alm whilst marvelling at the fragility of time.

Endon (Map 47)
Endon boasts a pharmacy and shop handy for the visitor moorings by Bridge 28. FINE FEATHERS farm shop offers organic foods, Calor Gas, teas, baking, crafts and ostriches. Tel: 01782 504460.

Denford (Map 47)
THE HOLLY BUSH - canalside Bridge 38. Tel: 01538 371819. A hugely popular Caldon Canal institution. 'Everything a country pub should be' according to the Good Beer Guide.

Cheddleton (Map 47)
Interesting village (St Edward's church has some fine Pre-Raphaelite stained glass) offering shopping and refreshment opportunities before you head into the interior.
Eating & Drinking
Three pubs, including the charming BOAT INN (Tel: 01538 360683) by Bridge 44, compete for your custom. CASTROS by Bridge 42 (Tel: 01538 361500) features Latin-American cuisine. There's a fish & chip shop too, about 10 minutes south along the A520 from Bridge 42.
Shopping
There are two convenience stores half a mile up the hill from the canal, and a post office by Bridge 42.
Things to Do
CHEDDLETON FLINT MILL - one of the great little museums of England. Tel: 01782 502907. CHURNET VALLEY RAILWAY - operates Sats, Suns, some Summer weekdays & Bank Hol Mons. Tel: 08707 666312 www.churnet-valley-railway.co.uk Preserved railway using steam and diesel traction. Much nostalgia plus an excellent way to facilitate a one-way towpath walk. Trip boat services connect with certain trains.
Connections
BUSES - services to/from Leek and Hanley also useful for towpath walks. Tel: 0870 608 2 608.

Consall Forge (Map 48)
Peace and tranquillity characterise Consall to such an extent now that it is hard to visualise the activity of the forges, furnaces and slitting mills which clustered here in the seventeenth and eighteenth centuries. Now, though, it is for the isolated BLACK LION (Tel: 01782 550294) that Consall Forge is best known - one of the most delightfully located pubs on the inland waterway system, it offers a good range of meals which may be enjoyed either in the cosy interior or the spacious garden where you can watch the boats and the steam trains go gaily by. Just a stroll away is CONSALL NATURE PARK and a wayside station on the Churnet Valley Railway. CONSALL FORGE POTTERY (Tel: 01538 266625) produces hand-thrown domestic stoneware.

Froghall (Map 48)
The 'village' consists almost entirely of what's left of the copper wire works, yet oddly enough this does not compromise the sense of isolation which pervades the otherwise unspoilt valley of the Churnet. Incidentally, copper cable from Bolton's sister factory at nearby Oakamoor was laid across the ocean bed to form the first Transatlantic telegraph in 1866.

The RAILWAY HOTEL (Tel: 01538 754782) offers food but there are no shops of any kind in Froghall. Buses (Tel: 0870 608 2 608) to/from Leek offer a handy service for towpath walkers as does the Churnet Valley Railway - Tel: 08707 666312 for train times and further information. Kingsley & Froghall station is currently the southern terminus of the line and its newly built station houses excellent tea rooms open daily throughout the tourist season. At the wharf a trip boat operates public excursions throughout the summer months - Tel: 01538 266486. Ice creams and drinks are available from the wharf house.

Hire Bases

ALVECHURCH BOAT CENTRES - Anderton, Trent & Mersey Canal, Map 2. Tel: 0870 835 2525. *www.alvechurch.com*

ANDERSEN BOATS - Middlewich, Trent & Mersey, Map 4. Tel: 01606 833668 *www.andersenboats.com*

ANGLO WELSH WATERWAY HOLIDAYS - Great Haywood, Trent & Mersey Canal, Map 13; Norbury Junction, Shropshire Union Canal, Map 36; Bunbury Wharf, Shropshire Union Canal, Map 43. Tel: 0117 304 1122 *www.anglowelsh.co.uk*

BLACK PRINCE HOLIDAYS - Bartington Wharf, Trent & Mersey Canal, Map 1 and Etruria, Trent & Mersey Canal, Map 8. Tel: 01527 575115 *www.black-prince.com*

CANAL CRUISING - Stone, Trent & Mersey Canal, Map 10. Tel: 01785 813982 *www.canalcruising.info*

CHALLENGER STEALTH - Market Drayton, Shropshire Union Canal Map 39. Tel: 01386 424386 *www.challengershare.com*

CLAYMOORE NAVIGATION - Preston Brook, Bridgewater Canal, Map 1. Tel: 01928 717273 *www.claymoore.co.uk*

COUNTRYWIDE CRUISERS - Brewood, Shropshire Union Canal, Map 28. Tel: 01902 850166 *www.countrywide-cruisers.com*

EMPRESS HOLIDAYS - Nantwich, Shropshire Union Map 37. Tel: 01270 624075 *www.empressholidays.com*

MARINE SERVICES (STOKE) - Etruria, Trent & Mersey Canal, Map 8. Tel:01782 201981 *www.stokeontrentmarina.co.uk*

MIDDLEWICH NARROWBOATS - Middlewich, Trent & Mersey Canal, Map 4. Tel: 01606 832460 *www.middlewichnarrowboats.co.uk*

NORBURY WHARF - Norbury, Shropshire Union Canal Map 36. Tel: 01785 284292 *www.norburywharf.co.uk*

Froghall Wharf

SHAKESPEARE CLASSIC - Barton Turns, Trent & Mersey Canal Map 17. Tel: 01926 314958

TEDDESLEY BOAT COMPANY - Penkridge, Staffs & Worcs Canal, Map 29. Tel: 01785 714692. *www.narrowboats.co.uk*

TRADCRAFT - Market Drayton, Shropshire Union Canal Map 39. Tel: 0121 531 0033 *www.tradcraftboats.co.uk*

VIKING AFLOAT - Staffs & Worcs Canal Map 30 Tel: 01905 610660 *www.viking-afloat.com*

WATER TRAVEL - Shropshire Union Canal Map 32. Tel: 01902 789942 *www.water-travel.co.uk*

Boatyards

ANDERTON MARINA - Anderton, Trent & Mersey Canal, Map 2. Tel: 01606 79642

ANGLO-WELSH - Trent & Mersey Canal Map 13 Tel: 01889 881711; Shropshire Union Canal Map 36 - Tel: 01785 284292; and Shropshire Union Canal Map 43. Tel: 01829 260638.

BARBRIDGE MARINA - Barbridge, Shropshire Union Canal, Map 43. Tel: 01270 528682

BARNTON WHARF - Barnton, Trent & Mersey Canal, Map 2. Tel: 01606 783320.

BARTON TURNS MARINA - Barton-under-Needwood, Trent & Mersey Canal, Map 17. Tel 01283 711666.

CALF HEATH MARINA - Calf Heath, Staffs & Worcs Canal Map 30.Tel: 01902 790570

CHAPEL FARM MARINA - Shardlow, Trent & Mersey Canal, Map 22. Tel: 01332 799561

DOBSONS - Shardlow, Trent & Mersey Canal Map 22. Tel: 01332 792271.

DOLPHIN BOATS - Stoke-on-Trent, Trent & Mersey Canal, Map 8. Tel: 01782 849390

ENGINEERING & CANAL SERVICES - Hoo Mill, T & M Canal, Map 12. Tel: 01889 882611

GREAT HAYWOOD MARINA - Great Haywood, Trent & Mersey Canal, Map 12. Tel: 07976 351920.

HASSALL GREEN CANAL CENTRE - Hassall
Green, Trent & Mersey Canal, Map 5. Tel: 01270
762266.

HATHERTON MARINA - Calf Heath, Staffs &
Worcs Canal, Map 30. Tel: 07831 153028.

JD BOAT SERVICES - Gailey, Staffs & Worcs
Canal, Map 30. Tel: 01902 791811.

KINGS BROMLEY MARINA - Kings Bromley,
Trent & Mersey Canal, Map 15. Tel: 01543 417209.

KINGS LOCK CHANDLERY - Middlewich, Trent
& Mersey Canal, Map 4. Tel: 01606 737564.

LONGPORT WHARF - see Stoke-on-Trent
Boatbuilding.

MARINE SERVICES - Etruria, Trent & Mersey
Canal, Map 8. Tel: 01782 201981.

MIDLAND CANAL CENTRE - Stenson, Trent &
Mersey Canal, Map 20. Tel: 01283 701933.

NANTWICH CANAL CENTRE - Nantwich,
Shropshire Union Canal, Map 42. Tel: 01270
625122.

ORCHARD MARINA - Higher Shurlach, Trent &
Mersey Canal, Map 3. Tel: 01606 42082.

OTHERTON BOAT HAVEN - Penkridge, Staffs &
Worcs Canal, Map 29. Tel: 01785 712515.

SAWLEY MARINA - Sawley, Trent Navigation,
Map 22. Tel: 0115 973 4278.

SHARDLOW MARINA - Shardlow, Trent
Navigation, Map 22. Tel: 01332 792832.

STOKE ON TRENT BOATBUILDING - Longport,
Trent & Mersey Canal, Map 7. Tel: 01782 813831.

STONE BOATBUILDING - Stone, Trent & Mersey
Canal, Map 10. Tel: 01785 812688.

SWAN LINE - Fradley Junction, Trent & Mersey
Canal, Map 16. Tel: 01283 790332.

VENETIAN MARINA - Cholmondeston,
Shropshire Union Canal, Map 44. Tel: 01270
528251.

WINCHAM WHARF CANAL CENTRE -
Wincham, Trent & Mersey Canal, Map 3. Tel:
1606 44672.

Trent & Mersey
near Swarkestone

How to Use the Maps

There are forty-eight numbered maps. Maps 1 to 22 cover the Trent & Mersey Canal in its entirety from Preston Brook to Derwentmouth; Maps 23 and 24 continue to Nottingham; Maps 25 to 27 cover the Erewash Canal;13 and 28 to 32 cover the northern half of the Staffordshire & Worcestershire Canal; and Maps 32 to 45 cover the Shropshire Union from Autherley via Barbridge to Middlewich. The Caldon Canal, a branch of the Trent & Mersey, appears on Maps 8 and 46 to 48.

Boaters navigating the FOUR COUNTIES RING should use Maps 4 to 13, and 28 to 45. Travelling clockwise around the ring - no matter where you start from - read the maps from left to right; anti-clockwise, right to left. For example, if you were to cruise the whole of the ring from Brewood in an anti-clockwise direction, you would turn first to Map 33 then 32, etc to 28; then 13, 12, 11 etc to 4; then 45, 44 etc back to 33. In any case the simplest way of proceeding from map to map is to turn to the next map numbered from the edge of the map you are on. Figures quoted at the top of each map refer to distance per map, locks per map and average cruising times. An alternative indication of timings from centre to centre can be found on the Route Planner inside the front cover. Obviously cruising times vary with the nature of your boat and the number of crew at your disposal, so quoted times should be taken only as an estimate. Neither do times quoted take into account any delays which might occur at lock flights in the high season.

Using the Text

Each map is accompanied by a route commentary describing the landscape and placing the canal in its historic context. Details of most settlements passed through are given

Information

together with itemised or summarised information of facilities likely to be of interest to canal users.

Eating & Drinking: Under this category we indicate a selection of establishments likely to be of use to users of the guide. We don't set out to make judgements in an Egon Ronay sense, but, generally speaking, the more detail we give, the more impressed we were with the place in question. It is desperately difficult to keep pace with changes at pubs and restaurants in particular, and we apologise in advance for any entries in the text subsequently overtaken by events.

Shopping in strange towns and villages is one of the great pleasures of canal travel. Under this category we try to outline the basic facilities for shopping in any given location as well as mentioning any especially interesting, unusual, quirky, charming, or simply timeless shops worth patronising for the experience alone.

Places to Visit: This is the age of the 'one-third A4 tourist attraction leaflet' and you may already possess material appertaining to every visitor centre within 50 miles radius of your itinerary. Nevertheless, we wouldn't be doing our job properly if we didn't outline attractions within easy reach of the canal, many of which seem all the more enjoyable when visited by boat.

Public Transport: Information in this category is quoted especially with the use of towpath walkers in mind, making 'one-way' walks using bus or train in the opposite direction. However we urge you to check to ascertain up to the minute details of timetables etc.

Towpath Walking

After years of official neglect and indifference numerous towpath improvement schemes have re-awakened public enthusiasm for walking beside canals. As an aid to walkers the maps in this guide depict the towpath in three categories GOOD can usually be taken to indicate the existence of a firm, wide, dry base suitable for comfortable walking and cycling; ADEQUATE hints at the chance of mud and vegetation, but can usually be considered passable; whilst POOR speaks for itself - diehards may get through, but it won't be much fun. By and large the towpaths of the Four Counties Ring and adjoining waterways are in good condition. There remain however, one or two 'black spots': in the vicinity of Knighton (Map 37); Woodseaves Cutting (Map 38); and Betton Cutting (Map 39).

Cycling

Cycling canal towpaths is an increasingly popular activity, but one which British Waterways - the body responsible for the upkeep of the bulk of Britain's navigable inland waterways - appear to regard ambivalently. At present it is necessary for cyclists wishing to use towpaths to acquire a free of charge permit from a British Waterways office - see opposite.

Boating

Boating on inland waterways is an established though relatively small, facet of the UK holiday industry. There are over 25,000 privately owned boats registered on the canals, but in addition to these, numerous firms offer boats for hire. These range from small operators with half a dozen boats to sizeable fleets run by companies with several bases.

Traditionally, hire boats are booked out by the week or fortnight, though many firms now offer ore flexible short breaks or extended weeks. All putable hire firms give newcomers tuition in oat handling and lock working, and first-timers oon find themselves adapting to the pace of ings.

Navigational Advice

ocks are part of the charm of canal cruising, but ney are potentially dangerous environments for hildren, pets and careless adults. Use of them nould be methodical and unhurried, whilst pecial care should be exercised in rain, frost and now when slippery hazards abound. The majority f locks featured in this guide are of the narrow ariety, but on the Trent & Mersey *east* of Burton-n-Trent they are widebeam and can fit two arrowboats side by side.

Mooring on the canals featured in this guide is s per usual - ie on the towpath side, away from harp bends, bridge-holes and narrows. ecommended moorings, of particular relevance urban areas, are marked on the maps with an pen bollard symbol. Long term moorings, usually quiring a permit, are indicated with a closed ollard symbol. Remember always to slow down hen passing moored craft.

urning - turning points on the canals are known s 'winding holes'; pronounced as the thing which ows because in the old days the wind was xpected to do much of the work rather than the oatman. Winding holes capable of taking a full ngth boat of around seventy foot length are arked where appropriate on the maps.

Winding holes capable of turning shorter craft re marked with the approximate length. It is of ourse also possible to turn boats at junctions nd at most boatyards, though in the case of the tter it is considered polite to request permission efore doing so.

Closures - known as 'stoppages' on the canals - usually occur between November and April when maintenance work is undertaken. Occasionally, however, an emergency stoppage may be imposed at short notice. Up to date details are usually available from hire bases. British Waterways provide a recorded message service for private boaters. The number to ring is: 01923 201401. Stoppages are also listed on BW's internet web site at *www.waterscape.com*

Harecastle Tunnel - a timetable of entry periods operates through the 'single-lane' tunnel at Harecastle on Map 7. In the interest of safety the tunnel is only open when manned by the tunnel-keepers who have offices adjacent to the north and south portals of the tunnel. operating times are as follows:

WINTER HOURS - November to mid-March. The tunnel is only open by appointment Mon-Sat. Telephone 01782 785703 or 01606 723800 giving at least 48 hours notice.

NORMAL HOURS - mid-March to mid-May and mid-September to end of October. The tunnel is open for passage between 8am and 5pm. *To be guaranteed a passage craft must arrive by 3pm.*

SUMMER HOURS - mid-May to mid-September. As above but open until 6pm. *For last guaranteed passage arrive by 4pm.*

Useful Contacts

British Waterways
Wales & Border Counties
Navigation Road
Northwich
CW8 1BH
Tel: 01606 723800

West Midlands Waterways
Peel's Wharf
Fazeley

B78 3QZ
Tel: 01827 252000

Fradley Junction
DE13 7DN
Tel: 01283 790236

East Midlands Waterways
Mather Road
Newark
NG24 1FB
Tel: 01636 675700

British Waterways operate a central emergency telephone service -
Tel: 0800 47 999 47

Inland Waterways Association

The Inland Waterways Association was founded in 1946 to campaign for retention of the canal system. Many routes now open to pleasure boaters may not have been so but for this organisation. Membership details may be obtained from: Inland Waterways Association, PO Box 114, Rickmansworth WD3 1ZY. Tel: 01923 711114 *www.waterways.org.uk*

Caldon & Uttoxeter Canals Trust
www.cuct.org.uk
Shropshire Union Canal Society
www.shropshireunion.org.uk
Staffordshire & Worcestershire Canal Society
www.swcs.org.uk

Acknowledgements

Many thanks to Brian Collings for the signwritten cover; to Toby Bryant of CWS; to Hawksworths of Uttoxeter and to Karen Tanguy. Mapping reproduced by permission of Ordnance Survey (based mapping) on behalf of The Controller of Her Majesty's Stationery Office. Crown Copyright 100033032.

Nine Good Reasons for Exploring the Canals with Pearsons

8th edition - ISBN 978 0 9 5491168 3

8th edition - ISBN 0 9549116 0 1

7th edition - ISBN 0 9549116 3 6

8th edition - ISBN 978 0 9 5491169 0

6th edition - ISBN 0 9549116 5 2

7th edition - ISBN 978 0 9 549 1166 9

6th edition - ISBN 0 9549116 2 8

3rd edition - ISBN 0 9545383 4 X

2nd edition - ISBN 978 0 9 5491167 6

Pearson's Canal Companions are published by Central Waterways Supplies. They are widely available from hire bases, boatyards, canal shops, good bookshops, via the internet and the Inland Waterways Association. For further details contact CWS on 01788 546692 or sales@centralwaterways.co.uk